In loving memory of my father, Peter.
I know you're reading this in another dimension
and I hope it makes you proud.

REMINGTON
DONOVAN

NUMEROLOGY

Hardie Grant

BOOKS

What is numerology?

THE UNIVERSE IS SPEAKING TO US, USING INFINITE LANGUAGES, AND NUMEROLOGY IS ONE OF THEM.

Numerology is not just about numbers: it is a way to translate one of the invisible languages of the universe. Numerology is synchronicity, and synchronicity is a sign of destiny. The method and practice of numerology opens up synchronicity, which, in turn, aligns with destiny.

Numbers exist in every facet of our lives. They come through as visible symbols of invisible communication. The world is numbers and the numbers are the world: from maths and science to metaphysics, music, design, architecture, geometry, coding – the list goes on. There is always a matrix unfolding. The possibilities are infinite and the numbers are infinite. The spiritual teaching is that every number is infinite and there is no difference.

The ancients and mystics have understood and utilised the wisdom of numbers since the beginning of time, and probably before time and time itself was a number. What I want to explore here is the mysticism and art of numerology, and its practical application. Numerology is often referred to as a science as well as an art, but don't worry: the most science we're going to do is simple addition (like 1 + 1 = 2), so don't allow that to bog you down. People often say to me, 'I'm just not good with numbers', but you don't need to be. Practising numerology is a fluid, artistic, creative, poetic, emotional and enlightening experience.

Something I really would like to emphasise here is that there is no need to make numerology an intellectual experience when you're reading this book and utilising the tools within it. I'll explain what the numbers mean, but these simple definitions are meant to be used as a starting point to launch your consciousness into the deeper realms of wisdom. As you practise numerology, the messages will come to you, and you will receive great insight. I cannot emphasise this enough: please make your practice fluid, artistic, enchanted and fun.

Numerology is a process. The answer is not always the goal. When you practise numerology, the channels within you start opening, enabling you to receive and expound wisdom. Through numerology, I've been able to assess and explore what would make a great career for somebody; I've been able to spot health issues; I've been able to see what the soul longs for, and to identify what kind of spiritual practice would most suit someone. It's not just about the definitions of the numbers: the practice of numerology itself opens up your consciousness, allowing it to become a receptacle for wisdom.

That being said, it is important to understand that numbers do hold certain vibrations. When you see particular numbers come up often in your life, you should pay attention. What are the vibrations of the number 5, for example? It has an energy of action and assertion. And what does that mean? Why are you seeing that number? Ultimately, numerology is used as a tool to better understand yourself, your soul and the world, and as a means to translate the language of the universe.

NUMBERS ARE EVERYWHERE

Many systems in many cultures use numbers, and most spiritual systems utilise numerology in some form. In this book, I'll be delving into a system known as 'tantric numerology', using that as the basis for how we come up with our own numerology charts. I'll also share my understanding of, and experience with, the mystical Qabalah to further explore numbers and their interpretations.

In this system, we will use 12 numbers: 0–11. This book will provide you with a great foundation in the wisdom of numerology, but I encourage you to explore how much further you can take each of these numbers in whatever spiritual tradition and spiritual practice you personally follow. Whatever it is, the practice of numerology can fit into it.

It's important to understand that these numbers, 0–11, encapsulate the entire cosmos. We have an infinite system here. Remember, each number is infinite, so there's no way one number could be explained in a few pages of a book. That's why I'll keep coming back to the point that this is not going to be an intellectual process. The definitions that I'm going to be providing and explaining are solely a launching pad for your own explorations. These are archetypal concepts, not unlike astrology, tarot, the I Ching or any other form of divination.

You don't have to be psychic to be a numerologist, but the more you practise numerology, the more psychic you will become.

I often say that even if you don't believe in numerology, it exists, simply because of the undeniable fact that numbers exist, in every single facet of our lives. For example, I write a lot about what the numerology is for any given year. So let's look at the year 2019. This is a '3' year $(2 + 0 + 1 + 9 = 12; 1 + 2 = 3 \ldots$ see, this is as scientific as we get). You have to remember that pretty much every day during the year of 2019, you're going to be exposed to that number. Whatever the year's numerology, your psyche and subconscious are going to be absorbing that energy field, and that alone leaves an imprint on you. It's not unlike the way that advertisements on billboards or in magazines are designed to imprint something into our psyches and subconscious and conscious minds: let's choose a higher elevated advertising and tap into the numbers.

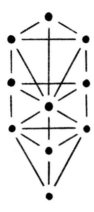

PRACTISING NUMEROLOGY

The practice of numerology is expansive and liberating. As with any type of practice, whether that's playing an instrument, competing in a sport, learning computer coding or juggling, the more you work with these numbers, the better you'll get at it. You will start to recognise patterns and consistencies, and gradually a reality will be revealed.

For example, as a numerologist, I can often recognise a prominent number in someone's chart based purely on how they move, dress and speak, and their overall vibe. Numerology leads us to that truth.

As we start to explore the meanings of these numbers and how they relate to your life and to your existence in the wider world, it is important to know that they can take on extremes. In numerology and Qabalah, it's all about balance and finding that sweet spot. When we get further along into the definitions of these numbers, you will see and understand the negative and positive energies that exist within each one. We reconcile numerology within ourselves, which is one of the keys to discovering our true power and potential. Numerology is meant to be a system of awareness of your soul, your incarnation, your true talents, gifts, abilities, lessons and challenges – and your destiny.

The practice of numerology shows us the tendencies, directions and patterns that naturally occur in our lives. It does not function according to the belief that we are stuck: we are not victims of fate. Fate is the concept that whatever is going to happen to us is already determined and cannot be changed, but nothing is written in stone. It is used to empower us and effect change in our lives. Numerology is a tool of destiny; your destiny is your highest incarnation and purpose. Whatever the number is, you can harness its virtues.

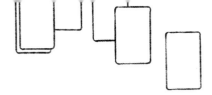

As you read this book, you will learn how to do your own numerology chart and the numerology charts of others. When you do these charts, allow the messages to come to you. You'll soon start to see greater, bigger patterns emerge.

It's very important to know that we use all of these numbers in our lives every single day, in almost every single moment. On some level, we're applying each number, its force and energies, into whatever it is we're doing. Even if you don't have a particular number in your personal numerology chart, it doesn't mean you don't use it in your life. Numerology is a journey of self-discovery.

Utilise numerology as a formula for success. There is no number that is better, greater or higher than any other number. Numerology gives you an understanding of your potential and how to maximise it in any situation in your life. As you get better and work with it, it becomes just like any practice. The definitions, keywords and energy fields of each number move you closer to and bring you more in tune with your purpose. When you actually put these methods into practice, it becomes a fluid, open, poetic, almost romantic experience between you and the universe – and this experience will open up your psyche and consciousness.

My story

My personal experience with numerology started at around the age of three. I received my first tarot deck (the deck I still use today) from my mother, who was given it as a tip while waiting tables at a vegetarian restaurant in Berkeley, California. I had no idea what the cards were, and treated them as a toy, but they became engrained on my psyche as I played with them. I took them out on an almost daily basis. Of course, I didn't discover this until much later, but Tarot ties into mystical Qabalah, which is the root system of the numerology I now use. So I see that first deck of tarot cards as my earliest introduction to numerology.

My formal practice of numerology began years later, when I began studying mystical Qabalah at the age of 19. The numerology that I practise today is the merging of what is known as tantric yogic numerology and mystical Qabalah. These systems aren't particularly different. I use the system of tantric numerology to come up with the chart. As for the interpretation, the numbers are the numbers, and they have the same meaning as they do in mystical Qabalah. You can go very deep with your interpretation and understanding, and it's something that's always expanding within you. Every single day, I gain new insight or uncover a new revelation about a number or numbers.

I say this to let you know that, regardless of how long you practise, or how good or natural at it you might be, numerology is an almost infinite process. Start where you are, and things will come to you and open up. Numerology is not a rigid process; it is a fluid one. It is one of the ways in which the universe communicates its secret language to you, and you can use it to unravel and understand that secret communication with the universe, even though sometimes it's obvious and the answer's right there in front of you.

I am now a professional numerologist, and by that I mean I do readings and incorporate numerology into the personal sessions I do with clients. Over the years, I've personally done thousands and thousands of readings. I work with numerology in some form or another every single day. What you may not realise is that you, too, are working with numerology, simply because you are surrounded by numbers: whenever you look at the time, the date, a number plate, an address ... The list goes on and on. Numbers are found in every facet of our lives. I hope that, with this book, you can start to decipher their message. What spiritual lesson do they have for you?

As I said earlier, my experience with numerology is rooted in mystical Qabalah and tantric yoga. As well as having the tarot cards as a three-year-old, I grew up as part of a spiritual community. I was born in an ashram, which is a spiritual centre. It was headed by a very highly respected teacher named Swami Satchidananda. From birth, I learned meditation, yoga and spirituality. I met very esteemed spiritual teachers from all over the world, from many different spiritual lineages and traditions. As a teenager, I really wanted to explore my own path, which led me to return to Tarot and explore it at a deeper level. I started reading books and doing tarot readings for a Sufi teacher. She was blown away and told me it was something I really needed to pursue. I was then fortunate enough to find a teacher in the Western Mystery tradition. The Western Mystery tradition is often referred to as Ceremonial Magick ('Magick' is spelled with a 'k' to differentiate it from stage magic). This is an ancient tradition that is handed down from teacher to student and taught in secret. Mystical Qabalah forms part of this tradition. This process has evolved over the last 30 years of my life.

After years of practising numerology in the Magickal tradition, I learned the method of tantric numerology and had a very profound experience as I discovered how closely related these systems are. I discovered many relevant, accurate and inspiring insights and clues about where I needed to develop and what I had to do to live my life to its fullest potential. I now practise a method that merges and harmonises Magick with tantric numerology. This is a method I was taught in my Kundalini yoga practice. Never in my wildest dreams did I think I would become a professional numerologist and mystic. But, as it turns out, living in Los Angeles, it's a marketable skill set and viable vocation.

When I meet with a client and I'm doing their numerology chart, what's coming through to me is generally focused on their highest potential and strongest skill set, but it's always accompanied by little things to be mindful of and lessons to be learned. It's my experience that my readings help activate the change. Remember, numerology is not about what is going to happen to us, but what we need to do. Numerology gives us real insight into this question, and highlights our natural talents and abilities. For many people, numerology confirms things they already knew, but were, for whatever reason, a little afraid to admit.

In this book, you will learn how to make a numerology chart in exactly the same way I do as an experienced professional numerologist. I receive insight and wisdom from students and clients all the time, and it's good to know that, although there are definitions of what the numbers mean, you're going to have your own personal experience and spiritual evolution, and through that you will develop a relationship of your own with these numbers.

How is numerology used?

STORYTELLING

Numerology is a form of storytelling. I once taught a numerology workshop that was attended by a friend of mine who is a writer, storyteller and animator. He has worked on some of the biggest Hollywood films and TV shows you've ever heard of. He was one of the best numerology readers in the class, because he could take the numbers and then turn them into a story.

Another time, I was working with an actress who sent me the birthday of a fictional character she was playing. I gave this fictional character a numerology reading, and it turns out, my findings matched up with what the whole story was about. Somehow, the scriptwriter had tuned into the numerology that was aligned with this character.

I work with numbers all the time and see countless shifts, whether those are changes to careers or relationships, or simply the individual developing a better relationship with their soul, their spirit and their true self. Helping people reach the stage where they recognise that they've always really known who they are and what they should be doing is a beautiful, powerful experience that I love with my entire heart and soul.

SOMETIMES A NUMBER IS JUST A NUMBER

Through Qabalah, I learned to look at numbers and see the different ways in which they show up – but sometimes, a number's just a number, and you can't get too caught up in it. For example, in the Magickal tradition, 22 is a very important and powerful number. It represents the 22 Major Arcana in the Tarot, and the 22 paths in the Tree of Life. There are also 22 Hebrew letters, which tie into a more advanced system of numerology called Gematria (see page 17). This is all just a long way of saying that I really like the number 22. Once, I was flying from New York to LA, and I decided to change my seat so that I could sit by a window. There were only a few window seats left, but I saw that 22A was available and thought, 'Oh, my God: 22. I love that number. And "A" is aleph in Hebrew. It's the Fool's card in the Tarot.' My logic was that this seat seemed much better than the seat I already had (18C), and so I switched. The thing is, I'd forced the situation: I'd overthought it, applying logic and my intellectual knowledge of the number 22 rather than allowing myself to be led by intuition. I couldn't wait to get on the plane, watch a movie and have an easy and relaxing trip.

Well, it turned out the screen for my seat wasn't working, so I couldn't watch any movies. I was sitting next to a guy in a stained tank top who smelled as if he hadn't showered in perhaps a week or two. He was eating old, brown bananas that had a very strong sulphuric smell and a soggy tuna salad sandwich. All I could do was sit there and smell him and what he was eating. And then, just to make things worse, the woman on the other side of him began eating really pungent teriyaki beef jerky. Soon my whole little section of the plane was just inundated by a combination of smells that should never be mixed, and I thought to myself, 'Okay. This is my lesson. Why did I get so gung-ho about taking up seat 22A?' Because, in my mind, it was a mystical number. But I should have just stuck with my original seat. When I looked down the aisle to seat 18C, the row was completely empty. I would have had it all to myself. That was just a little lesson that taught me not to get so caught up in things or force the situation. It's funny, looking back on it, and the situation was harmless, but it was still an annoying and unpleasant flight that, to this day, I have never forgotten.

Another time, I was shopping at my local 'bougie' market in Los Angeles, when a guy who knew I was a numerologist ran out to my car and flagged me down. He was very excited – almost frantic – and I thought something must be wrong. I pulled over and he said to me, 'Remington, your total came to $18.42. What does it mean?!'

I thought for a minute, then told him, 'It means I just spent way too much money on a fresh juice and bottle of water.'

As much as every number has meaning, and as fun as it can be to go down these rabbit holes, it's important to apply some common sense. Sometimes a seat is just a seat, and a receipt is just a receipt, and a number is just a number.

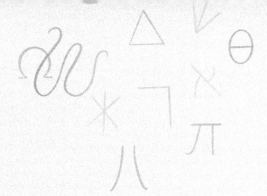

NUMEROLOGY IN CULTURE

As I have said, there are many different cultures and spiritual traditions, all with their own systems and symbols, and numerology appears in many of them. For example, there is Chinese numerology, there is yogic numerology and there is numerology used in Buddhism. Numerology is also used in ancient Hebrew, as well as Qabalah and Gematria, a practice involving the conversion of numbers and letters. I personally practise Gematria, and some of it ties with the methods we'll learn in this book. There's ancient Greek Gematria and numerology, and I'm sure it can be found in countless other systems, cultures and traditions. It's fascinating to think that numerology is used in all these different traditions all over the world, but the truth is that numerology is used by everybody, all the time. For example, it's rare to meet someone who doesn't have either a lucky number or a favourite number, and often they will have created their own story – their own mythology – around that number. Or it might be a playing card rather than a number. Playing cards, and tarot cards, too, are also systems of numerology. Many games tie into numerology and systems of numbers.

The numerology I teach is based on my experience of mystical Qabalah, which is a root system of numerology. Through years of doing that, it's very easy for me to look at other systems to see how they really align and tie in.

NUMEROLOGY IN NATURE

There's something within nature, and within both our individual psyches and the collective psyche of humanity, that gets a sense of what these numbers mean on a more spiritual and philosophical level. I'm often asked, 'Is numerology a construct? Are numbers a construct?' and I say no. Numbers and numerology exist in nature, whether or not we have recognised this. We are looking at what these numbers mean: the spiritual and philosophical teachings behind them. There's a saying: 'Was mathematics discovered, or was mathematics invented?'

Why do bees make honeycomb in hexagonal patterns? It so happens that the number 6 in Qabalah is attributed to yellow, and bees and honey are yellow. Roses are often attributed to the number 5, and you can break down some of the petals into sequences of five. Red, too, is connected to the number 5. When you cut a red apple in half horizontally, you'll see its core forms a five-pointed star. The Fibonacci sequence, known as 'the golden ratio', can be seen in everything from pineapples to the pyramids, from sea shells to sunflowers, from pentagrams to pine cones, tree branches, galaxies, hurricanes, DNA, human faces – the list goes on. This system of numbers, mathematics, geometry and science would exist whether or not we labelled it.

THE NUMEROLOGY OF DATES

Another thing I get asked about a lot is the numerology of dates. Is this a construct? Yes, the calendar that we use today is, on some level, a construct, but there are deeper spiritual teachings that say it's a construct that was designed from nature. The lunar calendar is 360 days, and the rotation of the Earth around the Sun forms a circle, which is 360 degrees. We may have turned a year into 365 days, but the roots of it still exist in nature. This is important to remember when we look at how different cultures and ideas tap into the essence of a number. Why is it that in American culture, the number 7 is almost always considered the most lucky number? Here in Los Angeles, there are convenience stores called 'Lucky Sevens' or '777'. If you just write that down and look at it, there's something there. The number 7 feels lucky, whether you're thinking of slot machines and gambling, or good fortune. And why, in pop culture, are we taught to fear the number 13? Many buildings don't have a 13th floor, for example, and Friday the 13th is considered a dreadful date.

What's interesting, though, is that in mystical Qabalah, 13 is a number of love, while in numerology you can add 1 + 3 to create 4, which is the number of love, compassion and mercy. So, somewhere, there's some sort of dark thought stream that has taken love, compassion, mercy and beneficence, and created fear around that. That's definitely something to think about. And what about 666? That's the number of the beast, found everywhere from the Bible to the names of heavy metal bands, but the deeper teachings of the number 6 are all about spirituality. In these contexts, 666 is actually a number that means the highest spiritual evolution of a human being. Perhaps, somehow, somewhere, that number has been demonised because people naturally fear their own spiritual growth.

The famous director, writer, creator and painter David Lynch is a numerologist. He's also very much into meditation. I've seen interviews with him where he talks about his own little made-up system of numerology and number plates, and how he knows whether or not one of his projects is going to get the go-ahead based on the numbers he sees on his way to the meeting. People in so many different cultures and professions utilise numbers in this kind of way. I'm not a gambler myself, but I know people who are actually very successful professional gamblers, and they often have lucky charms and their own lucky numbers. This is an energy field that they've tuned into, and for whatever reason, it seems to work out for them.

The number 108 is a very, very significant number in yoga. As a child growing up in a particular yogic lineage, all of the mantras and chants were done in sequences of 108, and mala beads in that tradition are all on strings of 108 beads. But I always thought it was very funny that a baseball also has 108 stitches. Is there a correlation? There must be.

Numerology as I teach it, and as it was taught to me, has a spiritual foundation that comes from the ancient Egyptian god Thoth. Thoth is the scribe of the gods and the keeper of the Akashic records. Thoth is depicted as having the head of an ibis, a bird that can stand for many hours on one leg. The ancients believe the ibis to be very contemplative, very meditative and very wise. Thoth is the god of all measurements, of all systems, of all sciences and all spiritual systems. Numerology is a spiritual system. Qabalah is a spiritual system. It's a spiritual method, and these methods come from Thoth. I was taught that the god Thoth receives this wisdom from the ethers, from the heavens, from divine spirit, from the divine creator, and bestows these gifts on mankind. With the energy of Thoth in your readings and your charts, you're working with an energy field that later on became the gods Hermes and Mercury. Numerology allows you to communicate with your highest and most divine self.

I hope this book will show you how to use numerology in your daily life, as much or as little as you'd like. Each number has equal value and merit: every number is infinite and there is no difference.

HOW TO USE THIS BOOK

I wanted to write this book to teach others to do numerology the way that I do numerology. It is clear, concise, direct and as simple as I can make it. Familiarise yourself with the traits of the numbers on the following pages, then turn to page 148 to learn how to create your very own chart.

A numerology chart is based on an individual's birthday and year. From there, we have a sequence and a series of placements and numbers that correlate with different concepts and teachings you can put into action to utilise in your life. It'll show your strengths, talents, and areas to work on.

Another aspect of this book is to have a basic understanding of the spiritual and mystical significance and definitions of each number. Numbers appear in our lives in many different ways. This book is meant to serve as a great reference point for these numbers, whether or not it is in your numerology chart.

GLOSSARY

You will come across the following terms throughout the book.
These are brief explanations, but it's well worth doing further
reading around these concepts, if your interest is piqued.

AEON OF HORUS —
In some traditions, this term represents an enlightened shift of consciousness for humanity that started in 1904.

AGE OF AQUARIUS —
Planet Earth goes through each house of the zodiac, and we are currently entering into Aquarius. Hence, this is the dawning of the age of Aquarius. Aquarius is about humanity, friendship and community.

AIN/AIN SOPH/ AIN SOPH AUR —
Terms used in Qabalah on the tree of life that mean nothing (ain), limitless (ain soph), and limitless light (ain soph aur).

ARC LINE —
The arc line is one of the yogic bodies, where it is said your destiny is written.

AKASHIC RECORDS —
The cosmic records of the entire universe.

GEMATRIA —
This is a system of numerology that associates numerical value to letters.

GOD —
The word God in this book is absolutely not intended to be an anthropomorphised, third party deity. But, at the same time, I don't want that word to interfere with what your personal relationship is with something that is higher. The loose idea of God in the context of numerology, at least, is higher consciousness, a higher order of the universe, a higher purpose than something that would transcend human intellectual comprehension.

And it's also something that is more experiential. To practise numerology requires no belief in God or a belief in a system or a deity, and can mix with whatever your own personal interpretation, religion, or spiritual practice is. So even an atheist can happily do numerology.

HERMETIC MAGICK —
Spirituality rooted in what is known as the Western Mystery Tradition and Ceremonial Magick.

I CHING —
A system of divination derived from Ancient China.

KUNDALINI YOGA —
A practice of yoga that awakens your kundalini energy.

PRANA —
Prana is the life force.

PRANAYAMA —
The practice of accessing life force through breath.

QABALAH —
Qabalah is a method and a process. It is a method of deepening your connection to the divine. Ultimately it's a method of deepening your connection to yourself and the universe around you. It is a system in which the hidden teachings and language of the universe will unfold, and within that system is the tree of life. One works with Qabalah in a very emotional, creative and artistic way. By doing numerology, or tarot, or astrology, or other systems, one is actually practicing Qabalah. This is very layered. You could spend literal lifetimes working with it.

TREE OF LIFE —
The tree of life is a foundation. It's like a universal key that many other spiritual systems have evolved out of such as numerology, astrology, and tarot, to name a few. I utilise the tree of life for one of the foundations of numerology. The tree of life consists of 10 sephiroth. You will find a tree of life diagram on page 9.

SEPHIRAH —
There are 10 sephiroth on the tree of life. Each Sepirah is an energetic area, or sphere, or plane of existence of the universe. Within each Sephirah, there are numbers, planets, colors, spiritual teachings, principles, philosophies, ideas and experiences.

TATTVAS —
Yogic term for the five elements of spirit, fire, water, air and earth.

WESTERN MYSTERY TRADITION —
This is a general term of the deeper, esoteric spiritual practice found in western culture.

YOGIC BODY —
There are said to be 10 yogic bodies (soul, negative mind, positive mind, neutral mind, physical body, arc line, aura, prana, subtle body, radiant body). These are different energy centres of your existence.

THE

NUMBERS

SOULFUL — IN TUNE — UNIQUE — ONE OF A KIND — SWEET SPOT

The number 1 is the 'soul body', and its spiritual teaching is 'heart over head'.

It represents the essence of ourselves and the truth of our souls. It is our undying connection to the source.

COLOUR	White
PLANET	Pluto
SEPHIRAH	Kether
DEFINITION	Crown
YOGIC BODY	Soul
CATCHPHRASE	'Heart over head'

AT A GLANCE

ONE IN ACTION

The number 1 is connected to the infinite creative source, which is why it's so creative. It is the first primordial point of creation that everything else stems from.

It has a very raw, pure, authentic, true essence, which is why it's linked to the soul. In a deeper spiritual sense, the number 1 really is the ability to always be in touch with not only the source of creation, your soul, but also with the highest divinity. This number gives you the ability to co-create with the universe. Are you at one with creation? Are you at one with your soul?

It is said that each of us has a unique soul, even though we're all connected as one soul to a greater soul, and it's ultimately all a connection with God. The soul is like our universal individual blueprint and our highest, purest identity. As we start to master this number, we come into contact with such a powerful aspect of ourselves that we discover a truth, honesty and reality that are almost untouchable. When we learn these lessons, we come into a very powerful, very soul-satisfying, enriched existence.

The number 1 creates things with an all-knowing, even if you don't know that you know it. With 1, there's no separation. It is all there is. It is the zone. Whether you are working at a computer, knitting, cooking, reading a book or riding a bike, whatever it is, you get into a focused zone and find satisfaction and purpose.

Keep asking yourself, 'What's true to my soul? Where am I at one with my soul? Where is my soul at one with everything else?' It's like that old joke where the Buddhist goes to the hot dog stand and the man asks him, 'What would you like, sir?' The Buddhist says, 'Please make me one with everything.' It's that sense of merging. It's really simple if you just think about it like this: the number 1 is about being at one with that source and that energy field. It loves to create.

The real emotional satisfaction of the number 1 can come from purpose and co-creation with divinity. But to put it in a simpler way, it's like having a nice life.

The number 1 is like being 'in the zone'. Whether that's cleaning the house, doing the dishes, playing music, etc., we have all experienced that feeling of being in flow, focused and in a really good groove. There's a deep, pure sort of satisfaction that is found in the number 1, as we connect with our highest selves and our divine source: with God, the universe, or whatever. If someone is channelling the energy of number 1, then that person, that artist, that creator is displaying something deeper, something more real. Their connection to their highest self can come through, whether they are writing, painting or whatever else they do to create.

When we utilise the number 1, we are tapping into the true essence and purity of ourselves, unaffected by ego or the illusion of the world. It is the truth of our reality.

In Hermetic Magick, oneness means there's one universe that operates in all these multifaceted, incomprehensible dimensions, and vibrations. But at its core and its source, it's all one vibration, and there are just different frequencies. So, as I write to you here, a part of my energy field and a part of your energy field are totally connected.

In Qabalah, the number 1 is Kether, meaning crown, which is the first Sephirah on the Tree of Life. The spiritual teaching of Kether is the first spark of manifestation. Kether represents our highest purity, meaning it is us in our most unadulterated, uncorrupted state, without outside influence. Its colour is white.

The planet of the number 1 is Pluto, which is the planet of high destiny. In astrology, it represents what your soul wants to learn in this incarnation.

We sometimes hear people say, 'That person has a lot of soul', perhaps in reference to an artist or musician, and we understand this to mean that the person has access to the truth of themselves, and that they're able to take that soul and co-create with the Creator.

The number 1 is very artistic, which doesn't always have to relate to actual art. As well as things like painting, dancing, singing and drawing, people can be artists in many different fields, and have many different 'artistic' abilities. Whether you're a gardener, an accountant, a lawyer or a cleaner, it is about doing any task and anything that's in front of you with creative intent.

ONE IN REFLECTION

The lessons of the number 1 have to do with the heart and the head. The key lesson of number 1 is learning to come into your ability to follow your heart. The possible downside of number 1 is that it can be over-intellectualised, a little too heady, and you can find yourself blocked, or overthinking your way out of what should be an enriched, emotionally heartfelt existence. Don't think yourself out of a wonderful life. The other negative side number 1 can be found in places where you apply too much heart. Are you spending your life just trying to capture everything that feels good?

We co-create with that. Follow your heart and soul, not your head. Heart over head. The head plays an important role, but when you use only your head and your logical thinking and your human brain (which is infinitesimally small compared to the universe), you're going to sell yourself short. If, however, this number is balanced and in the right alignment, you are living a soul-satisfying experience and can enjoy a fulfilled heart, without overthinking getting in the way.

So a lot of the lessons about the energy of 1 are really to do with following your heart, but also about going deeper than just the heart chakra, to the essence and heart of you and your soul. When we use the number 1, we're really tapping into this divine source of creation.

There is a strong lesson of authenticity and purity here. It's not that we don't draw inspiration from others, but when it's not us doing it, then what is? The number 1 is about managing that balance of truly getting into the zone with our highest selves. That's the simplest way to put it. Keep it simple. Be yourself.

LESSONS FROM ONE

The number 1 is about just being in flow, being in the moment, being in that groove. We've all had those days where everything just starts flowing, everything just starts working out. You find a parking spot right in front of every business you go to. The doors are always just opening as you approach them. You're always running into the right person, in the right place, at the right time. You're manifesting the powerful energy of a strut.

That's why it's very important to utilise the number 1 as something creative. Whatever you're creating in the world, whether it's a sandwich or an artistic masterpiece, that energy is the same.

In Magick, there's a teaching that tells us to do everything with excellence. When you really start to do things with a mastery and an excellence, it becomes very easy and accessible to be in that zone. You're always on target, and you never miss your mark.

With the number 1, you're really tapping into the true power and strength of your soul. The art of life is the alchemy of existence. In Qabalah, this is our spiritual practice. Our entire lives should be in the zone of spirit. We must strive to let go of the ego — the illusions of our false selves — and attain an existence in which we are inebriated with divinity and spirit.

When I explore these numbers, I always like to reference things that come up, so there's a sort of fluid and artistic free association. Try this with the number 1. What are some of the first things that come to mind when you see the number 1? For example, I always think of that song 'One is the Loneliest Number' (and we'll see how that can even come into play with the number 2, which is all about fulfillment). I also think of the song 'The Groove is in the Heart' by Deee-Lite. It also makes me think of Obi-Wan Kenobi from Star Wars saying, 'I'm number one'. The winner is always number one. You're first, so it's important that the real message is to be a winner. When we are one with the number 1, we are one with our souls.

If you keep seeing the number 1, maybe it's time to focus on yourself, or perhaps it's time for a great new beginning. It could be a confirmation that you're in the groove or a message that you need to be more authentic and creative.

INTERPRETING ONE

VIRTUES

Focused, purposeful, intentional, true,
authentic, consolidated, creative,
empowered, independent, have integrity

VICES

Thinkaholic, untrusting, isolated,
disconnected, scattered, confused,
disingenuous, poser, stunted

MOTTOS

'I create with creation.'

'I start from the heart.'

'I am myself.'

'I'm in the zone.'

'Create, don't compete.'

FAMOUS ONES

Princess Diana, Marilyn Monroe,
Justin Bieber, Billie Eilish, Morgan Freeman

FULFILLED — CONNECTED — CONTENT — JOYOUS — LOVEY-DOVEY

The number 2 is the 'negative mind', and its spiritual teachings is 'longing to belong'.

The negative mind is the open, receptive part of ourselves that longs for fulfillment; what are you filling it with?

COLOUR	Grey
PLANET	Uranus and Neptune
SEPHIRAH	Chokmah
DEFINITION	Wisdom
YOGIC BODY	Negative mind
CATCHPHRASE	'Longing to belong'

AT A GLANCE

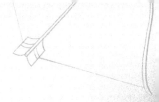

TWO IN ACTION

The number 2 is about receptivity and open-mindedness. It's ultimately about pure love and strong connection to the divine. The open shape of the number 2 wants to embrace the entire world with a huge hug. It is the number of friendship and connection. When we utilise this number in our lives in its highest aspect, we have a wonderful love affair with our souls, the world and divinity. When we are fulfilled and overflowing with the satisfaction of spirit, this is where a lot of success resides.

The power of the number 2 is the ability to receive and make connections that will enhance our lives. For example, let's say you're trying to get a job at a specific company. If you have a strong connection with the number 2, it will use that desire to belong. When this longing to belong is directed in the right way, it will easily create the opportunities we need to make connections. The key is to be an open, fit receptacle to receive the things you want.

The number 2 provides a good energy field for building and nurturing relationships and family, making wise connections, and creating a life of fulfillment. The negative mind works in conjunction with the positive mind, which is the number 3. Like the aperture of a camera lens, the number 2 opens up, adjusts and assesses any given situation. It makes no judgement. It takes no action.

On the Tree of Life, the number 2 is Chokmah, which means 'wisdom'. Chokmah is the second Sephirah, which is the first highest identity of creation. There are two planets attributed to the

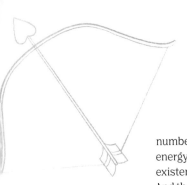

number 2 — Uranus and Neptune. Uranus is the energy of change. What we had in all creation and all existence was the number 1, which was everything. And then it broke away into the image of itself to form the number 2. Uranus wants to break away, break things up, and do things a little differently. Neptune, meanwhile, is the ability to merge back into your soul and into that exalted existence.

The number 2 creates an environment of inclusion and unity. It's a very social number. It loves love, and it is a great number for relationships, including family, friendships, community and romance. The number 2 is very open to new possibilities. It's an energy that likes to say yes and is willing to go with the flow.

The number 2 is intuitive (even the sound of the word 'two' is in intuitive). Since it is open to a flow of possibilities, when the number 2 starts to say yes to opportunities, it can create a tremendous amount of fulfillment in your life. All numbers are like magical powers. The number 2 helps with your psychic abilities. It helps with the true manoeuvrability of your intuitiveness because it opens you up to saying yes, and knowing what the right thing is for you.

Think of the number 2 as this magical hug: what are you hugging? What are you receiving? What are you putting in that negative space? What are you fulfilling and what are you putting in your mind? Pull it in. Be open to it. Be a little more spontaneous. Get into a nice flow with your life. Say yes to new possibilities, and watch how you can really move the energy forward.

TWO IN REFLECTION

What is the downfall of the loving, community-orientated, trusting energy field of 2? Well, when there's so much longing and desire for fulfillment, we will often look beyond ourselves to fill our desires – sometimes to a destructive end. We live in a society that loves to pump us full of outside stimuli that promises fulfillment, whether that's drugs and alcohol, relationships, sex, shopping, food, scrolling on social media all day, etc. Be mindful of the outside sources that seem like the solutions to fill your void. The number 2 can lead to some serious FOMO (fear of missing out). This is what 2 really has to assess.

It is the number of allowing and opening up to all possibilities. The negative side of this is that it can make us way too trusting and too open, and lead us to say yes to every single possibility without any consideration of whether it might be destructive or harmful. The key lesson is to know how to stay open and fluid while retaining a certain level of discernment. The motto for 2 is to say yes; the lesson for 2 is to understand when to say no. This number can also be taken to negative extremes by making us highly distrustful, leading us to become shut off or defensive.

As much as number 2 loves love, relationships and connections, the downside of this can be that you become so dependent on that outside source of fulfillment that the other person becomes your be-all and end-all. The number 2 also loves to fall in love quickly, which means you can take this negative tendency from one relationship to the next. It's no coincidence that the second chakra is often associated with fulfillment, addiction and sexuality.

If your number is 2 and you don't have a solid connection with your soul, there's a risk that these outside factors will give you a false feeling of fulfillment.

LESSONS FROM TWO

How do you use the number 2 in the world? Well, think about that empty space, and what it is that you want to receive. What would you like to connect to? Perhaps it's a new job, perhaps it's a new relationship or a new community. Maybe you want to move somewhere else. Maybe you want a new set of dishes for your home. Whatever the case, the empty space of 2 can receive it. It is a very powerful number when it comes to the magic of receiving.

The number 2 represents soft, ambiguous, abstract thinking. Let's say you want a job, or there are certain clients you want to attract, or there's a particular industry or firm that you would like to position yourself in. The number 2 can soak it up and bring it in. If you use this number wisely, you can receive anything. It creates a wonderful community. When you have that working in your favour, you can say yes to miracles and possibilities. With the number 2, anything is possible. It's a number that can navigate the world with ease and satisfaction.

If you keep seeing the number 2,
the universe might be telling you that
it's time to open up a little.

What can you say yes to?
It could mean that you're in flow, that
you're making connections and building
friendships and community – or maybe
you're meeting that special somebody.

INTERPRETING TWO

VIRTUES

Intuitive, trusting, fluid, open-minded, loving, connected, community-focused, receptive, fulfilled, satisfied

VICES

Suffers from FOMO (fear of missing out), too trusting, co-dependent, indulgent, shut down, closed off, frigid, dissatisfied, despairing

MOTTOS

'Yes.'

'I am enough.'

'I am open to new possibilities.'

'I am trusting, I let go, and I flow.'

'I have what I want. I have what I need.'

FAMOUS TWOS

Mahatma Gandhi, James Baldwin, Kurt Cobain, Spike Lee, Cher, Larry David, Dr Seuss

AMBITIOUS — OPTIMISTIC — BUILDER — LEADER
BRILLIANT — ANALYTICAL — INTELLIGENT

The number 3 is called the 'positive mind'. It is assertive, direct and gets things moving. This links to the third chakra, which is called our 'command centre'. It's where we find the energy to function powerfully in the world.

COLOUR	Black
PLANET	Saturn
SEPHIRAH	Binah
DEFINITION	Understanding
YOGIC BODY	Positive mind
CATCHPHRASE	'Devil or divine'

AT A GLANCE

THREE IN ACTION

In Qabalah, the number 3 is Binah on the Tree of Life, which means 'understanding'. Its colour is black and its planet is Saturn. Saturn is the builder and the taskmaster. Saturn says, 'I'm going to roll up my sleeves and I'm going to get the work done', and the number 3 will do just that. It gives us the courage, confidence and power to build and take action on the things that we want in our lives. When your 3 game is strong, you're going to be optimistic. You're going to suit up, show up and do your thing. The number 3 just keeps going. Saturn is the great 'adulting' planet, so the number 3 gives you 'adulting skills'.

Somebody with a really strong and righteous connection to the number 3 will have courage. It is the number of an entrepreneur and a boss. The number 3 is a natural leader. Even if you don't have a 3 in your numerology, you have to stand in that courage in order to be a leader. You have to know when to take action, how to be decisive and how to move forward. Use this number wisely. Come into your confidence, your power and your courage. Come into your right place. The number 3 is a bold leader, especially when it's in its highest aspect.

The number 3 gives you great power and great ability. When your 3 game is strong, you're confident: you're a leader, and you're brilliant. The

mind, when used in its best way, gives us access to a divine brilliance and logic. We utilise the dichotomy of the numbers 2 and 3, which represent opposite ends of the spectrum, to step into the neutral mind and create balance. As the number 2 represents the 'negative mind' and open space, this dynamic works hand in hand with the positive mind of number 3, which is more assertive, precise and action-orientated. Remember that number 2's negative mind is a little more fluid, intuitive and creative. Number 3 is very logical. When you use these two numbers together, you have a great formula for being open, creative and balanced (as opposed to just being so logical you've lost sight of abstract thought).

The number 3 is a go-getter and it wants to achieve great things in the world. It's a wonderful number for success and building. If you feel like you need to step up, become more mature and confront life on life's terms, the number 3 can help you do that. The number 3 is more about the projection so it can take action. It is a very brilliant number: the number of optimistic courage. When our connection with number 3 is on point, we truly have command, power and authority in the world.

THREE IN REFLECTION

The negative side of the number 3 can be seen in disempowerment or a lack of courage. If this number is taken to extremes, we might see someone who is always asserting too much power and aggression: somebody that's 'too bossy', for example.

At times heavy and intellectual, the number 3 is highly analytical, which does serve a good purpose and function in the world, but another of its potential downfalls can be 'the paralysis of analysis'. This can be seen when we overthink every single possibility to the point of inaction, meaning what was the number of action becomes the number of inaction because we've become stuck in trying to find the perfect answer. If you are overly analytical, you lose sight of the bigger picture, and that energy can definitely leave you feeling stuck and blocked. So remember to use this number to help you think about a logical plan, and then just go for it. You can manoeuvre and adapt as you go because you're still going to use your negative mind to allow things to happen a little more fluidly. Don't overthink it. Go for it. It takes focus, and Saturn is the planet of focus. The negative side of Saturn is that it can be the planet of imprisonment, leaving you feeling trapped and stuck where everything is hard. So the key to the number 3 is use it for clear-minded, divine brilliance.

If you're getting into a negative spiral, sometimes it's just a matter of needing to take action in order to get your head out of that downward trajectory. For example, if you're reading or watching the news, it's easy to spin out. The number 3 likes to spin out. So assess where you're overthinking and where you're tripping up, and take action to fix it.

Sometimes the number 3 can go to the very extreme, where everything seems to be steeped in some sort of dread and paranoia. I sometimes joke that 3 has a keen sense of dread because this thinking, action-orientated mind may be overcalculating the worst-case scenario in everything. For example, if someone important to you sends you a message, saying 'Hey, we need to talk later', and your immediate reaction is to think 'Oh no, what's wrong?' Falling into a number 3 spiral might lead you to think: I'm going to get fired. I'm getting demoted. I'm going to get dumped. I think a lot of us have probably been there. Sometimes just getting a little bit of information allows the 3-focused mind to really overprocess. This is why we link the number 3 with the idea of 'Devil or divine'. Are you opening up to that divinity, or is your mind getting bogged down by the details? After all, the devil's in the details. So, are you just overthinking everything?

Ask yourself, 'Where am I overthinking my way out of what could be a fluid, intuitive situation?' We have an objective, rational, logical mind, and then we have an intuitive mind. As yogis, magicians and spiritual practitioners, we are taught to use both. When the positive mind of the number 3 is used correctly, the discernment it brings us ultimately strives for balance. In Qabalah, we look for this balance.

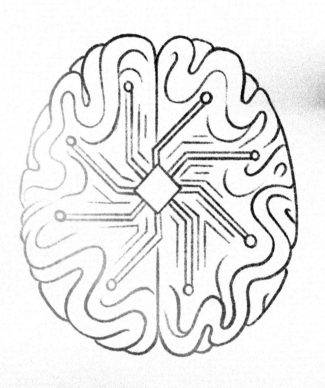

LESSONS FROM THREE

The number 3 can be too three-dimensional, leaving little to no room for abstract thinking. The highest strength of this number gives us the power, courage, drive, intelligence and action we need to build. Don't be limited by the biological functions of your brain. Our minds are infinite, and therefore serve as a tool for the infinite. When your positive mind is strong, it has access to a whole new level of genius and power.

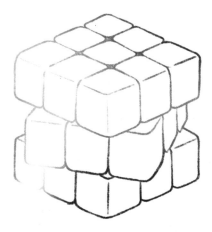

If you keep seeing the number 3, maybe it's a sign to step into your leadership role, get more professional, and do the work. It could mean that things are coming to fruition, or it may be a sign that you need to tone it down a little bit and ease up.

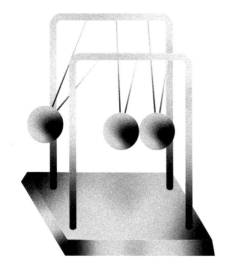

INTERPRETING THREE

VIRTUES

Professional, able to project, brilliant, optimistic, authoritative, strong, confident, determined, disciplined, have gumption and grit, analytical

VICES

Hard-nosed, uptight, rigid, buttoned-up, overly analytical, fails to take action, meek, ineffectual, too bossy, authoritarian, pedantic, paranoid

MOTTOS

'Yes, I can.'

'I am confident and courageous.'

'I share my strengths, not my weaknesses.'

'I have the courage to take my ideas and put them into action.'

FAMOUS THREES

Queen Elizabeth II, Winston Churchill, Arnold Schwarzenegger, Marlon Brando, Abraham Lincoln, Gal Gadot

MIRACULOUS — BLISSFUL — ABUNDANT — DIPLOMATIC
KIND — OBJECTIVE — HUMANITARIAN

The number 4 represents the 'neutral mind': a space of total access, openness, acceptance, and the ability to assess honestly and impartially the truth of any situation. The number 4 is the heart centre.

COLOUR	Blue
PLANET	Jupiter
SEPHIRAH	Chesed
DEFINITION	Mercy
YOGIC BODY	Neutral mind
CATCHPHRASE	'Openness'

FOUR IN ACTION

In Qabalah, the fourth Sephirah on the Tree of Life is called Chesed, which translates as 'mercy'. Its planetary alignment is the planet Jupiter and its colour is blue. The number 4 represents real compassion, acceptance and the ability to assess truth and its reality.

Are you able to accept yourself? Are you able to accept the parts of yourself that maybe need a little work? Are you able to accept the parts of yourself that are awesome, and recognise what you're really good at? Now remember, you are, of course, totally awesome. But it's good to assess ourselves honestly and truthfully, without self-criticism or self-judgement, and identify where we would like to improve. The neutral mind of the number 4 gives us the ability to assess who we really are. This number gives us the ability to be open and see the truth. Before, we were using the openness of the number 2, the negative mind, and the action of the number 3, the positive mind. The number 4 can reconcile these energies really well.

The number 4 is blissful existence. When you get to that level of acceptance and peace in every moment in your life, you will discover so much coming through you and your heart centre. The beautiful lesson of this number is really the ability to accept both ourselves and other people exactly as we and they are, letting go of the need to try to control or influence others. We're at peace with who we are; we're at peace with other people. And from that high space, many opportunities come to us.

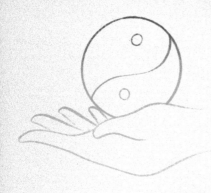

This number doesn't take things personally, so a great place to start with is yourself. Try not to take yourself so personally; try not get so caught up in your own thoughts, ego and feelings.

Now, the Jupiter energy of the number 4 is found in spiritual teachings of wisdom, miracles and expansion. How do you achieve a miracle with the number 4? It gives you the ability, through radical self-acceptance, to be exactly where and who you are in that moment. It's very much like the old teaching: 'Be here now.' When you absolutely trust that where you are is exactly where you're supposed to be, you'll always be in the right place at the right time. Jupiter is the planet that is trying to work it out for you. It's the planet that's trying to make things easy. So, don't complicate this one. Keep it simple. Stay very open-minded. Assess reality. Don't take it personally.

When you're moving through the heart, in that truly centred space of compassion, the universe will start to provide opportunities for success. This is a great way to change the frequency. The number 4 is also a number of high Love, with a capital L. While the number 2 is all about connection, and potentially romantic love, 4 is the high Love, the high compassion, of the universe.

How do we grow in our lives? We expand through our hearts and we grow through miracles. Once you tap into that, things will change. You'll move away from fear, anxiety and regret, and you can truly begin to live a blissful existence by being here now, in this moment. It's like the saying goes: 'The present is a present.' The number 4 gives us the consciousness of the present and therefore gives us the consciousness of adaptability.

This number says, 'Okay, here's the reality of the situation.' Once we understand this, a strong number 3 can come in and say, 'Okay, now I know that, I will adapt. I'll move forward.'

Adaptability, at a really core level, is actually about forgiveness – because adaptability simply says, 'Oh, this situation's just changed. I'm not going to freak out. I'm going to be cool about it. And I will make the necessary changes.'

FOUR IN REFLECTION

The number 4 is the truest, purest, most open-minded consciousness. What is the opposite of that open and loving number? It's being judgemental, resentful and shut off to possibilities. This number can be close-minded and judgemental, both outwardly and inwardly. This negative side of the number 4 can also be seen in a tendency to take everything personally. Try to let go of anxiety about the future. Remember: 'Worrying is praying for things we don't want.' Keep hold of your compassion. Keep hold of your love. Hold that heart space to the world. One of the most poignant key lessons of the number 4 is to forgive ourselves for everything that we have judged to be wrong or imperfect. Let it go. Live in the moment and do the work that's in front of you, as accurately and neutrally and righteously as possible.

Because the number 4 has a more passive energy, it can be enabling, complacent, ineffectual and lazy. The negative side of this number might accept something as 'good enough', saying, 'Oh, this will do', 'It is what it is,' and 'It won't make a difference.' Ask yourself: are you holding yourself back from success? Are you enabling others to walk all over you?

But remember, 4 is the number of miracles. How do you invoke and create the miracle? By getting into that '4 space'. Get into that wise, compassionate, heart-centred space of you. Say to yourself: 'I'm in the moment. I've let go of all my preconceived notions of how my ego thinks everything should turn out.' If things don't turn out as you expect, you can find yourself thinking that you have failed. But that means too much 3 energy, right? Thinking, thinking, overthinking. 'Oh, I've failed, I've messed it up.' Let the number 4 come in and clear it.

Allow the miracle to work for you. The number 4 gives us the miracle of starting afresh from a place of wise compassion for ourselves and our true hearts. If we just open up the real courage of our hearts and try to assess what could create a better opportunity, we will tap into the real frequency of miracles. The planet Jupiter wants to grow and expand, and it wants this to be easy.

LESSONS FROM FOUR

A key lesson of the number 4 is the importance of forgiveness – think '4-giveness'. We have to learn to forgive the past. We have to learn to forgive others. And, most importantly, we have to learn to forgive ourselves. If you find that you're the type of person who has a tendency to hold on to resentments and never move beyond the past, if you're still angry over things that happened to you as a child, you must realise that each soul has to work through personal experiences. It's very important that we all learn how to come into the mastery of the number 4 and discover our ability to live in the moment, forgive the past and move into a blissful heart space.

The number 4 is a very open number, and one of its lessons is about not to take things so personally. If you are down on yourself, thinking, 'I'm a failure, I'll never do this, I'll never make good money, I'll never have a partner', the number 4 gives you the opportunity to say, 'It's a choice now.'

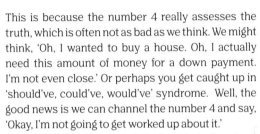

This is because the number 4 really assesses the truth, which is often not as bad as we think. We might think, 'Oh, I wanted to buy a house. Oh, I actually need this amount of money for a down payment. I'm not even close.' Or perhaps you get caught up in 'should've, could've, would've' syndrome. Well, the good news is we can channel the number 4 and say, 'Okay, I'm not going to get worked up about it.'

Sometimes, just knowing what obstacles stand between you and a goal is enough for the universe to start clearing the way. So don't hide or find yourself overcome by fear. Step into the nice, calm, cool and collected state of mind that number 4 can bring us.

I always think of each of these numbers as giving us a new magical ability. The number 4 gives you the power to accept who you are in that space, in that moment, and to trust that you have everything you need and are exactly where you're supposed to be. The compassion, acceptance and radical self-acceptance that the number 4 brings can give you so much strength and ability as you move through the world because you're no longer caught up in the narrative of what you think you're supposed to be. And when you get to that frequency, the universe is going to work with you. There is an alchemical process when you move through the heart: you let go of what you're afraid of and what holds you back.

If you keep seeing the number 4,
the universe is probably asking you
to deal with a situation: to deal with
life on life's terms and assess reality.
Maybe it's asking you to be more
compassionate or look at
the truth without
making things
personal.

INTERPRETING FOUR

VIRTUES

Truthful, accepting, loving, compassionate, open-minded, fair, righteous, diplomatic, kind, sharing, beneficent, giving, civil

VICES

Lazy, enabling, passive, boring, prejudiced, greedy, doormat, pushover, selfish, 'drives in neutral', judgemental, oppressed, opinionated

MOTTOS

'I am cool, calm and collected.'

'I am open to the truth.'

'I assess what's best.'

'Allow the miracle.'

'I live in a loving, compassionate, beneficent universe.'

FAMOUS FOURS

Stevie Wonder, Barack Obama, Rosa Parks, Sun Ra, Swami Satchinanda, Meghan Markle, Jeff Goldblum

TEACHER — TRAILBLAZER — WARRIOR — INITIATOR
ENFORCER — EDITOR — ATHLETE

The number 5 represents the physical body. It is the teacher, disrupter and editor. The number 5 is a very assertive, aggressive and corrective energy field. It knows how to use force and how to use action.

COLOUR	Red
PLANET	Mars
SEPHIRAH	Geburah
DEFINITION	Strength, severity
YOGIC BODY	Physical body
CATCHPHRASE	'The teacher'

FIVE IN ACTION

If you look at a five-pointed star, also known as a pentagram, it is actually a symbol of a human being. Think of the famous Vitruvian Man by Leonardo Da Vinci. The human body can be arranged in the shape of a star, which is one of the reasons that the number 5 is attributed to the physical body.

We've gone through the soul body (1), the different bodies of the mind – negative mind (2), positive mind (3) and neutral mind (4) – and now we've reached the number of the physical body. We're incarnated into our bodies, in corporeal form, to learn karmic lessons. The number 5 is a teacher. What else does a teacher do? A teacher corrects, balances and restores order. The number 5 is always about restoring balance. There is a yogic teaching about the five tattvas, which are the five elements (fire, water, air, earth and spirit). You always want to have these energies in balance – think of Ayurvedic medicine and Chinese medicine, where one might have 'too much' fire or 'not enough' fire.

It is the assertive, corrective nature of the number 5 that brings things into order. A teacher is someone who can correct a deficiency, resolve a deficit, and bring order, balance and righteousness into a situation. Does this mean somebody with a lot of 5s in their chart has to be a teacher? No, but it does suggest that this is a person who can correct a situation. This number also represents the throat chakra, which is responsible for communication. Again, think of a teacher. What do they do? They communicate and correct. The number 5 is about

communicating what is right and having the ability to speak up about your needs and wants, and so put things into action.

The number 5 is a pointy number. It has a very dynamic, powerful and fierce energy. In Qabalah, the number 5 is the sword, and the sword is meant to cut through illusion. This number wants justice. Think of it like weeding your garden. The number 5 goes in and removes whatever is getting in the way of your growth and destiny. The teacher helps clear the way and cut through obstacles.

Number 5 is the warrior. On the Tree of Life, it is called Geburah, which means strength and severity. Its planetary attribution is Mars. Mars is power, right action, vigour, instinct, empowerment, assertion and war. For example, let's observe the Pentagon, which functions as the war offices of the United States of America. To be honest, I couldn't think of a better shape for a building that relates to war.

Mars is raw energy and raw power, but this energy and power need to be sustained, and to be used for good: think right action. Do the right thing for the right reason, and use the energy of 5. It is also the number of destruction. Now, we can use destruction in a positive way, to clear away, obliterate and then liberate. The number 5 is a powerhouse.

It is the number of action. It's a go-getter. It's a quick starter. The key to the number 5 is taking that little burst of energy and using it to sustain and have more impact on the world.

The energy field of 5 sparks a new beginning. It takes initiative and creates change. A teacher is one who often pokes and provokes in a way that can inspire you. The number 5 is like a little jab. It's that fire under your butt that gets things going – which is why 5 is the number of activation.

The energy of 5 also knows how to say no. That's a big lesson from the number 5: no is the new yes. Get comfortable saying no. This number knows what it wants, and it knows what it doesn't want. The number 5 is great at setting and communicating boundaries. It's okay to assert yourself, say no and set a boundary, but you don't have to be a jerk about it. With a little bit of practice, you will realise that assertion isn't aggression.

This is an assertive number. It says, 'Hey, I'm going to take action.' The number 5 is the energy that gets us out of bed. It's like the alarm clock that wakes us and shows us it's time to head to the gym.

The number 5 can balance a situation because it takes away the things that don't serve the righteous order of whatever that situation is. We always need an energy that can cut away and clear. It's like peeling and chopping vegetables: you cut away what you don't want.

Remember, the number 5 is like an editor. Whether you're editing a film, a book, a magazine, or anything in your life, when your connection with 5 is strong, you can decide what to cut away, identifying what doesn't serve the real essence and the soul of what you're editing (whether that's your existence, a project or a particular situation). It is considered a number of sacrifice. What are you sacrificing? You're sacrificing that dead weight. When your connection with 5 is strong, you can clear away so many obstacles and really empower yourself.

FIVE IN REFLECTION

The negative side of the number 5 can be overly assertive, aggressive, temperamental, rash and impulsive. It could also manifest as someone who does not stand up for themselves, does not communicate their wants and needs, and does not set boundaries with other people.

For example, this could be someone who can't bring themselves to tell their boss: 'I really need Tuesday off because I have to go to an event.' If you don't ask for the day off, you don't get the day off. You might become resentful and angry towards your boss and your job because you weren't given what you never even asked for. This can leave you stuck with anger and resentment because you end up internalising it until you become subconsciously and consciously aggressive towards yourself on a deep-seated level.

The energy of 5 can be used to clear out the obstacles that hinder our success. The negative side of that clearly is going to be vengeance: destruction for the sake of destruction, violence for the sake of violence. The *Art of War* tell us: 'Never go to battle for the sake of going to battle.' This is the downfall of the number 5: it can be a petty tyrant. It's important to keep that in balance. In order to use the energy of 5 appropriately, you have to stay calm, cool and collected, while simultaneously being empowered and action-orientated, and comfortable acting instinctively and asserting yourself.

The aggression of the number 5 often comes

through resentment, and resentment often happens when one doesn't communicate one's needs: it festers and lingers, and eventually you lash out, becoming violent on some level. This doesn't mean you're physically punching a hole in the wall, but a diminished 5 is an angry, rash energy field, and it's inherently destructive. So, if you find you're easily getting annoyed and pissed off, your 5 is probably a little out of balance. The key is always respond and never react.

In relation to Mars, the number 5 is about desire. Mars is passion and action, so this can mean going for what you want. There's nothing wrong with that. The danger comes when you want something so badly that you lose sight of everything else.

LESSONS FROM FIVE

Two of the great lessons we can learn from the number 5 are: 'I can communicate what I want' and 'I can clear through those channels with communication; assertion doesn't have to mean aggression.'

A real teacher helps activate something within you and for you. Whether it's a latent talent or your spiritual practice, a teacher gives you the tools to enhance your ability and become more in touch with your soul. They ignite your talent and guide you in how to use it.

If you keep seeing the number 5, the universe might be telling you to step into your role as a teacher more. Or maybe it's asking, what you can disrupt in your life? Where do you need to assert yourself? Where do you need to become more empowered? It's time to wake up and embrace your destiny.

INTERPRETING FIVE

VIRTUES

Action-orientated, disruptive, able to edit and teach, assertive, energetic, passionate, fierce, inspired, able to destroy obstacles, go-getting

VICES

Rash, hot-headed, buzz-killer, tyrannical, violent, destructive, oppressive, fearful, truculent, domineering, vindictive

MOTTOS

'No.'

'Say yes to no.'

'I am comfortable asserting myself. It's easy and natural to me.'

'Getting what I want is totally fine.'

'I clear the fear.'

FAMOUS FIVES

Albert Einstein, Booker T. Washington, Tony Hawk, Che Guevara, Kobe Bryant, John Coltrane, Neil Armstrong

VISIONARY — APOSTLE — PERSON OF PRAYER — NETWORKER
HARMONIOUS — CENTRED — MANIFESTOR

The number 6 is referred to as a 'person of prayer'.

In Qabalah, the number 6 is connected to meditative intelligence, and represents the harmonising beauty of the cosmos.

This number has a very reverent, respectful and spiritual energy field.

COLOUR	Yellow
PLANET	Sun
SEPHIRAH	Tiphareth
DEFINITION	Cosmic beauty
YOGIC BODY	Arcline
CATCHPHRASE	'As above, so below'

AT A GLANCE

SIX IN ACTION

The six-sided star, also known as a hexagram, is used by many spiritual traditions, including Hinduism, Judaism, Christianity and Hermetic Magick. This star is a symbol of the union of the macrocosm with the microcosm, which infuses divinity into the 'mundane realm'. As above, so below.

The arcline is the sixth yogic body, and looks almost like a halo. It's an energy force that sits above each of us, in the area above our heads. You cannot see it with the physical eye. We hold a lot of divinity within this energy field, and it is also where our destinies are written. You may have heard people say, 'Oh, this person is going to be a success. It's just written on their forehead.'

When we utilise the number 6, we can rewrite our destinies. How do we do this? Well, 6 is the 'person of prayer', so why not use prayer? Just think of prayer as setting an intention and directing that energy towards some sort of higher good, whether it's the universe, or God, or whatever you would consider the higher part of yourself to be. You don't have to get caught up in what you're praying to. Prayer sets a positive intention and opens up channels that allow the energy of miracles into your life. The number 6 has access to this energy: it harmonises and brings divinity to every situation.

This number creates a sacred space. Many people I have worked with who have prominent 6s in their numerology charts are interior designers – this number brings with it an intuitive knowledge and a sense of where things should go. It's like feng shui, or a feeling that creating a nice, orderly space allows for something more divine to come through. My dad always said to me, 'The spirits like a clean room' – this was his way of getting me to tidy up my bedroom. The energy of the number 6 could be used to organise and arrange a retail space. Huge firms are built around analysing retail stores and the ways in which people navigate these spaces, paying attention to how the arrangement of a space and the placement of objects within it can affect our psyches. Have you ever walked into a really nice restaurant where everything is in perfect alignment and harmony? The candles are burning, the tables are lined up straight, and the place settings are meticulous. This sense of spatial harmony is a great example of the number 6. Start to see how you can create more sacred spaces in your life: how you can create a harmonising flow and beautiful, divine order in everything that you do.

In Qabalah, the number 6 is the sixth Sephirah, Tiphareth, which means 'beauty'. This refers to the cosmic beauty and harmony of the universe. The number 6 is the connector and the unifier: it connects the macrocosm with the microcosm, the divine with the mundane. It connects God to human. It can connect anything larger with something smaller. Think of, say, an agent in Hollywood who has access to all the potential jobs and roles available in the industry. They may connect those projects to a writer, an actor or director. The same goes for a recruitment firm. They have access to more information about available jobs, and they can connect individual jobseekers with the information they need.

I know someone who works for a medical recruitment firm. Essentially, they connect a qualified person with qualified positions. They're uniting the macrocosm of the jobs available in the medical field with the microcosm of one individual, one potential employee. So on that level, we can see that 6 is not only a connector and networker, but also brings a high, divine energy into every situation.

The number 6 is a very sacred number. It creates order and likes to align everything with something more divine, bringing with it a spiritual essence. It's also the number of devotion and dedication. When used in a very high, dignified way, it is dedicated to your spiritual evolution. This number enables you to have a clear conduit to the divine and tap into a higher degree of energy, which you can then bring it into your life.

The colour of the number 6 is yellow, and it is represented by the planet of the Sun (in astrology, the Sun is considered a planetary body). The sun is the centre of the Solar System, and all the planets orbit around it. Therefore, 6 is the number of orbits. Think about when NASA puts a satellite into orbit: it takes on a life of its own and gets into a nice, natural flow as it follows a natural orbit. Think about other examples of orbits. Within our bodies, for example, we have the glandular system and our blood circulation – these have an orbit that flows through and around the body. The number 6 is your centre: it's the core of your soul. But it's also the centre of the universe. It's the centre of the Tree of Life. The number 6 represents the ability to get into orbit, to get into a flow with a higher order and the higher abundance of the universe. The sun represents light and strength and God, and number 6 connects us to that light.

On a practical level, it's like a sacred placement of objects, but 6 enters into another zone and can get into a cosmic flow. It will put things in orbit. And 6 has a follow-through. It is a very diligent number. It wants to show up and do its due diligence and its service, to do the work and get something into an orbital flow.

The number 6 represents your spiritual practice. That doesn't always mean you have to go to a temple, church, meditation group or yoga centre in order to be aligned with 6, although those do relate to this number. One of the easiest ways to connect to 6 is through prayer and meditation. It's not about praying to Jesus or Guru Ram Das or Ganesh. The 'who' is pretty irrelevant. No matter who or what you direct your prayers towards, this is really about stating an intention and a direction to the universe. Meditation, meanwhile, brings you

to a still point where you can connect with something higher, whether that's the higher consciousness of your brain, your soul, your frequency, God, the universe, divinity, etc.

The number 6 always strives towards the orbit of destiny. This is where your 6 will become very empowering and very strong. It is where our destinies are written: the Akashic records, which mystics see as the records of the journey of each soul.

SIX IN REFLECTION

As 6 is the number of orbits and divine flow, it can get completely stuck in an unchangeable rut. If you're in the same orbit, doing the same things in the same way all the time, you're going to feel stuck. Think about any areas of your life in which you might feel stuck. Where has the inertia of the orbit become heavier than your ability to change?

Since 6 is the number of consistency, diligence and follow-through, its negative side is inconsistency and a failure to follow through. This, combined with the idea of being stuck in a rut, brings to mind the saying, 'Same shit, different day.' If, for you, every day is the same thing, day in and day out, it's time to look at your number 6.

With this number, we are really looking at the patterns and cosmic flow of your life.

When an orbit is working for you, you might think, 'Hey, I'm in the zone, I'm in a flow, I've got things going.' It's can feel a bit like you have the ability to switch to autopilot. But the risk is that that orbit can just become the same thing, over and over – not flow any more, but repetition. And so you become complacent, and you just exist in the inertia of your orbit. If you feel like your life's in a rut, or you just feel like you're doing the same thing over and over and over and you're getting nowhere, it's time to look at your 6.

As I explained earlier, 6 is the arcline where our destinies and fate are written. Fate is an orbit of our soul that we can't break: it's like having a life where we're not empowered to makes changes. Your destiny, however, is your highest life, and through spiritual practices, you can alter your destiny and rewrite it. You can shift from fate consciousness (what will happen to me?) into destiny consciousness (what must I do?). Use the number 6 to align with the beautiful orbit and elevated vibe of your soul.

LESSONS FROM SIX

As spiritual practitioners, we believe in the idea of destiny as the individual choosing to open up to their highest potential. In Magick, we call it your true will. It's your highest purpose and the highest expression of your divine self. The number 6 can manifest: it has access to this through the arcline. The arcline is where the records are kept.

The Magickal teaching says, 'One is born with an allotment of different things, from money, to breaths, to foods, to sports cars.' The list goes on, depending on what you are meant to experience. But with this energy of 6, we can change all of that, so we don't have to be the victims of our own prescribed fate. The key with the number 6 is to know how and when to activate change and rewrite your destiny.

The number 6 represents harmony. If you look at patterns of 6 – honeycomb, crystals, snowflakes – you can sense the harmony of those cells and structures. If your 6 is off, it's time to think about where you might be losing your centre. What are you orbiting around? Are things in your world messy? Scattered? Are you orbiting around your fear and anxiety? Are you orbiting around somebody else's concerns? Number 6 teaches us that we need to orbit around our centre, our own sun.

The energy of 6 gives us a great opportunity to open up our destinies and create change in our lives. One of the practices of 6 is to literally write things down: write down what you want, what you'd like to change and how you'd like your life to be. Moving from fate into destiny, that's the number 6.

If you keep seeing the number 6, the universe may be sending you a message to get centred, find focus from within and listen to your higher self. It could also be a sign to make changes, create a spiritual practice, get organised and be consistent.

INTERPRETING SIX

VIRTUES

Sacred, dedicated, reverent, diligent, harmonising, wise, enchanting, spiritual, prayerful, meditative, wise, contemplative,

VICES

Lazy, easily distracted, irreverent, complacent, disconnected, scattered, lacking in follow-through, inconsistent, erratic, irregular, mercurial

MOTTOS

'I change within to change the world.'

'I am the creator of my destiny.'

'It's always an inside job.'

FAMOUS SIXES

Dalai Lama, Martin Luther King Jr.,
Bob Marley, Steve Jobs, Frida Kahlo,
Leonardo da Vinci, Bob Dylan, Andy Warhol

VICTORIOUS — PROSPEROUS — LOVELY — ENCOURAGING
CHARMING — ARTISTIC — BEAUTIFUL — SENSUAL

The number 7 represents 'the aura'. The number 7 has a sweet, gentle, caring energy field that goes into a situation and makes everything better, nicer and brighter. It is also one of the most sensitive numbers, and very much an empath.

COLOUR	Green
PLANET	Venus
SEPHIRAH	Netzach
DEFINITION	Victory
YOGIC BODY	Aura
CATCHPHRASE	'Elevation'

SEVEN IN ACTION

In Qabalah, the seventh Sephirah on the Tree of Life is called Netzach, which means 'victory'. This is attributed to the planet Venus. As much as Venus represents art, creativity and sensuality, it's also the planet of feeling secure on a very deep level. Venus is beauty. Venus is nice things and rewarding relationships. Venus is true value and self-worth. If you value yourself, you will create a lot more prosperity in your life. You'll feel more secure in the world, and this security will enable you to help others value themselves, too.

The number 7 is the number of the perpetual upgrade, which can translate into finer things and a very high, prosperous, evolved energy field. The number has a very charming, pleasant energy that other people like to have around them, whether in a work environment, a social environment, or whatever the situation is. This number makes everything that much shinier, prettier and sweeter. It's a very lucky number.

The number 7 really loves to help others and has the energy of an emotional healer. That's one of the reasons it's called the platform for elevation. One simple example of this is that those with number 7s in their numerology chart help others feel good about who they are. Often, I'll see that manifest as they become counsellors, healers and therapists, or take on similar roles. To put it very simply, you can say, 'Wow, 7 just makes the world a nicer place.'

This number is connected with the aura, which represents each person's personal energy field. Your aura extends out of your physical body as your own little safety zone. A lot of the core elements of the number 7 relate to our sense of security and our ability to feel safe in the world. When we have that, we create a safe space around us that will make others feel good and nurtured. There's a teaching in Magick that says you can't have a lot of holes in your aura, so you've got to stay vital. You've got to keep your personal energy and your personal space vital, as this will help you accomplish more, which will, in turn, give you greater power to help others. So stay sensitive, but always be strong and know that vulnerability is empowerment.

Think of the number 7 as an upgrade, an energetic payday, to help you feel safe and secure. This number encapsulates the energy that we keep in more delicate and private spaces. I joke and call it the 'energy in the bedroom'. That doesn't mean that it has to be sexual – it just means it's cosy, it's private. It's like wearing a luxurious robe or being in bed with thousand-thread-count sheets. It's soft and gentle.

This number wants to feel good, but it also wants everything around you to look good and taste good. Don't fall into the trap of thinking that a designer purse or a brand new sports car or a pair of shoes or a sexy new lover will be what gives you the fulfillment that you're looking for, though. Keep that in balance. When used appropriately, the energy of this number can lead to tremendous self-worth and self-value. It's important to know that you can have an abundant, prosperous life. Be guided by your own self-worth. This number strives to look into a situation and ask: 'How do I improve it? How do I make it better?'

SEVEN IN REFLECTION

The negative side of this number can be overextending yourself when helping others, to the point of forgetting about your own needs. This number can sometimes be a bit of a 'people-pleaser', leading you to say yes to things because it ultimately wants to help. However, don't overextend yourself to the point where you are draining yourself. If that happens, you're not actually helping others because you're destroying yourself. Help yourself first. Remember the oxygen mask rule when flying: 'Put on your own mask before assisting others with theirs.'

This number's planet is Venus, which rules Taurus and Libra. Taurus is about 'stuff', I often joke, while Libra can be about other people. This can lead to you get overly wrapped up and concerned about other people and how you can make their lives nicer.

This number needs to learn how to be an empath without getting attached to the outcome of other people's problems. It's okay to feel everything, but if you're going to think it's all about you and your ego, you may run into feelings of insecurity and lack of love. You need to have true love and true compassion in order to feel and sense other people's issues. True compassion is acceptance, and part of this is accepting that you can't always fix everyone else's problems.

Negative sides of this empathetic energy may manifest in you being too open and too sensitive, and feeling unsafe, insecure, threatened, and/or overly vulnerable. The number 7 is like a sponge that absorbs bad vibes and energy. It will often be more sensitive to external influence.

As this number has such an empathetic, sensitive energy field, you have to be mindful of what you're consuming. From mass media to food to intoxicants to other people's vibes, 7 feels everything. Things that have a tremendous effect on the aura include foods, places, energies and intoxicants. Different forms of media, too, can have a significant effect.

There's a teaching that says, 'Whoever has the biggest aura wins.' When your aura is strong, fortified and powerful, you're not going to allow others to affect you. Working with all things that have to do with cleansing, purity and vitality are important with this number. An out of balance 7 may have tremendous food sensitivities, get bogged down by other people's bad vibes, and are too affected by their external environment: where they live, where they want to live or where they are. You know those people that are always seeking or insist that they have to live in a particular sort of environment, whether it's the country or city, whether they need to have a garden, or see sunsets, or be by the water? On a positive note, none of that matters. It's about knowing what's right and what charges your aura. This number can take on negative qualities when you're overly concerned with outside influences in order to bring strength and vitality to the inside. The number 7 is often the energy of a nutritionist or therapist because they understand what make us feel good and secure, and what keeps our energies upbeat, light, bright and positive.

LESSONS FROM SEVEN

Even in modern numerology, 777 is considered a very lucky number because people just pick up on its 'upgrade' energy field. So how do you work with the number 7? What can you make better in your life? What can you improve on?

We always have this sweet, nice, sensitive energy within us, and we protect it with our auras. So we have to strengthen our aura game. What affects the aura? For one thing, intoxication creates a lot of holes in the aura, and leads us to become way more vulnerable to other people's energies, influences and entities. I'm not saying this in any judgemental way – it's just a Magickal fact. Some people are incredibly sensitive to this, while for others it's not as intense. It's up to you to recognise whether this is an issue for you. Whether it's media, foods, intoxicants, medicines or herbs, be aware that your aura is a sponge. It absorbs everything.

Every time you're connecting with other people – when you shake their hands, or you hug them – just know there's a little auric energy exchange. That's fine: we live in the world, we're going to end up exchanging energies and auras. With too much of that, though, our auras can become depleted, and we become weak, insecure and more vulnerable. A strong 7 helps on every level: emotionally, energetically, physically and mentally. It carries a strong presence and leaves you secure and uplifted. The energy of 7 is a prosperous upgrade of everything in your life.

Even if you don't have a 7 in your numerology chart, it's still good to ask yourself where you might be being overly sensitive, then learning how to manage that. The number 7 is a very vulnerable number. It is emotionally sensitive and empathetic. It's important to know that being sensitive and being vulnerable is all part of the process.

To be good numerologists, we have to be sensitive and attuned to things that aren't necessarily seen by others. The key is to recognise this as a strength and not a weakness. By strengthening your energy and aura, you can use sensitivity as something empowering rather than letting it bog you down.

If you keep seeing the number 7, the universe might be asking you what in your life could use a prosperous upgrade.

Or maybe it's telling you to do something nice for yourself and someone else.

Or perhaps it's a message to look closely at what you're consuming.

It could also be a sign that you're gonna get lucky.

INTERPRETING SEVEN

VIRTUES

Elevating, abundant, artistic, tasteful, epicurean, sensitive, sensual, sexy, sweet, improver, able to understand true value and self-worth, charming, helpful, generous, tender

VICES

Vapid, insecure, decadent, empathetic, people-pleasing, charmless, prudish, selfish, emotionally vampiric, defeated

MOTTOS

'Victory!'

'Elevate and celebrate.'

'I am safe and secure.'

'Prosperity is time, love and money.'

FAMOUS SEVENS

George Harrison, Kate Moss, Picasso, Elton John, Billie Holiday, Will Ferrell, Ravi Shankar

VIII

HEALING — POWERFUL — REGENERATIVE — ENERGISED
INSPIRATIONAL — MOTIVATED — ENDURING

The number 8 represents the prana, the life force of the universe. This is a very active, energised, powerful number.

It is fearless. It gives us the energy to do anything we want. It is regenerative and resourceful. When we have more energy, we have more options.

COLOUR	Orange
PLANET	Mercury
SEPHIRAH	Hod
DEFINITION	Splendour
YOGIC BODY	Prana
CATCHPHRASE	'From finite to infinite'

EIGHT IN ACTION

The number 8 is one of the high-energy, powerhouse numbers. It is raw, pure life force. It gives you the ability and energy to do whatever it is that you want to do.

This number's colour is orange, and it is attributed to the planet Mercury. Mercury is considered a healer in the old mythology. Mercury is not just about communication: it's also linked to our high, brilliant, scientific mind function. By adding more life force to 8, in a regenerative and sustainable way, Mercury helps us find solutions and cures, whatever the situation is.

If you have more energy, you have more options. If you have a lot of energy and vitality within you, you can hike up a bigger mountain without getting out of breath. If you're in shape, you can just keep going. It's like the Energizer Bunny: your battery is charged, you're in shape, you're feeling vital, you're feeling strong, you're well-rested. You're ready to go. So what, exactly, are you charging?

While science believes that oxygen is what the body needs for life, the mystic believes that what is needed is prana, the unseen healing energy that often attaches itself to oxygen. Through the breath, the prana is what really gives us vitality in life. Regardless of all that we know, the energy of 8 is the energy that fuels our lives, our souls, ourselves, and every part of our existence. If you're vital and energised, you're going to be able to walk, jog, run and conquer any mountain. This concept can also be applied to money. The more money you have, the more options you have. The number 8 is one of the best numbers for money, energy and the things that give us fuel in life.

Money is a necessary part of the world in which we live, and it is what fuels and maintains our existence. When we tap into the restorative power of the number 8, we become a magnet for more money, prosperity and success. There are some simple things you can do to open yourself up to the power of this number. As the number 8 is the pranic body, you can access it through breathwork exercises or, if you're a practitioner of yoga, anything related to pranayama. No matter what your spiritual practice or tradition says, every single human being has to breathe in order to live. Every single creature in this worldly dimension has to utilise prana and breath in order to survive. As we get more oxygen, it will start to empower us. Tell yourself: 'I'm well rested, I'm clear, I'm empowered, I am energy.' You're going to do whatever you want in the world.

The number 8 is also the number of the healer because when you have access to the infinite life force of the universe, everything that you're doing is creating life. This number loves to be of service to others. As you tap into that vital life force, you become fearless. You become powerful enough and strong enough to really help others, to be of service, and to bring others into their own power and vitality. This is a strong number. Channelling the power of the number 8 can leave you feeling prepared, charged, enthusiastic, energetic, powerfully charming and ready to go. If you have your energy in order, you are able to help even more. We should all have enough energy to allow us to expand, share and help others. That's the true blissful experience of the number 8. People with the number 8 in their numerology chart can get really good at something because they put in the time and energy to work it out.

This is a very enthusiastic number. It's like dopamine, or a sort of spiritual caffeine. It's ready to go. So, how can we always be invoking the powers of life force?

EIGHT IN REFLECTION

The downside of number 8 is not being energised enough, or being unable to tap into the resources you need to have a sustainable existence. Do you have enough? Do you get paid enough? Are your needs met? And can you have more than what you need? Yes, you can, and 8 is one of the frequencies that helps you attain it.

This number is an adrenaline junkie: it's burning the candle at both ends; it's full steam ahead. We're going for it, and then, all of a sudden, at some point: bam, crash, we're exhausted. Have you ever had a high-intensity job, or been in a situation where you've had to exert lots of adrenaline, lots of energy, and then found yourself feeling just drained and dead to the world? Those are things to look at with a deficient 8. It might mean you're burning out, blowing your fuses, and going too hard.

I often see things like adrenal fatigue or just fatigue more generally, in people with an unbalanced 8. They may feel that they never have the energy to move forward and take charge of their lives. This is where some sort of conscious breath work really becomes paramount. There are yogic teachings telling us that just 11 minutes of conscious breathing a day can make a huge difference.

Energy is money. Whatever you put your energy into, that will grow. If you put your energy into prosperity and confidence, that is what is going to grow. What fears do you need to look at and overcome? Are you frugal? Are you a money hoarder? How much energy are you exerting in order to save a few bucks? What is that really worth?

Another negative side to the number 8 is being unprepared. Have you ever had a day where you oversleep, and then when you do wake up you realise you forgot to charge your phone the night before? You have a really important phone call to make, perhaps for a new opportunity, and you have to go to a meeting all at the same time. You have to drive, but forgot to put fuel in the car, so now you'll be delayed even more by stopping for fuel. Your phone is about to die, and you remember that you took the phone charger out of the car a few days ago. And now, you have to pay for the fuel, but your credit card is declined because you're waiting for a payment to go through. The negative side of 8 leaves us without the vitality, preparation and/or energy we need to manoeuvre in this world.

As you start to work on this, do the little things first. Make sure your phone is always charged. Look into energising and revitalising foods. Get a grip on your finances. Stop overspending. Know that if you have 8 in your chart, you actually have the ability to make a lot of money. You're always prepared for any situation.

I often see a deficiency in the number 8 manifest as being in debt in some way. It's like waking up on the wrong foot, as the saying goes. You're always playing catch-up. Your energy field doesn't understand how to hold on to resources. And it isn't just in terms of energy reserves and money where you might find yourself 'in debt'. This number can be a time debtor, leaving you showing up a day late and a dollar short. Perhaps you are always putting something off, saying you'll do it another time, sweeping it under the rug. And next thing you know, years have passed, and you never took care of it.

Look at areas of your life where you don't take into consideration the amount of time it is going to take to do something. It's being late, never on time, not having a sense of time and putting things off until later.

LESSONS FROM EIGHT

As I have explained, 8 is a great number for money. Money is the manifestation of life-force energy in a more three-dimensional realm. If you have more money, you have more options, and you are more empowered. In this way, we can see that 8 is a very resourceful and regenerative number.

If you were a hunter-gatherer, you would need that life-force energy in order to have the endurance and power needed to hunt and survive. The number 8 gives you the opportunity to say, 'What is giving me more life? Or what is, on some level, slowly killing me?' I know that sounds dramatic, but just what is stopping you from having more empowerment and zeal? This number adds more life to life.

Think of 8 as resourceful empowerment. Anything that gives you more resources leaves you feeling energised and empowered. Again, 'resources' can mean a lot of different things – it doesn't just have to mean money. Having the resources you need makes life easier. The number 8 tries to give you the chutzpah and energy you need to live life without a lot of fear.

One of the great lessons of this number is to start to recognise and trust in the idea that we live in an abundant universe, and there is enough for everybody, including you. The number 8 sees no need to compete. Always create, don't compete. This number is vital, strong and empowered. It gives you

the energy to create – even the sound of '8' is in the word 'create'. It can be a really inspiring number. I see a lot of people in the finance world who have strong 8s. So look at your relationship with all of those things and see where you can be more empowered.

How do you add more life to the situation? We know that this number can be the life of the party, full of zeal, but how do you add this power, and how do you help others access that vitality? The number 8 loves to be of service and help others. There's nothing the 8 energy would like to do more than help you feel energised and empowered, and to share that feeling and bring that into the lives of other people.

In the game of pool, it is the eight ball that wins – but if it's played wrongly, the eight ball can end the game. This is an example of 8 as life force, but also death force. Which are you utilising when you channel the energy of 8?

I always say this jokingly, but the number 8 comes up a lot in the language we use around drugs and other substances. For example, I don't do drugs personally, but I'm told that cocaine is sometimes sold in 'an eight ball' – and that's a very high-energy, active substance. And although I only mention it in a joking way, it's interesting to think about why we've used the number 8 in these ways – because, on some level, some part of us understands that 8 is high energy.

If you keep seeing the number 8, the universe might be asking you:

'Where are you focusing your energy?

How can you be more vitalised?'

It could be an encouraging sign that you need to tap into your energy flow and push through. It might be a message from the universe that says, 'Hey – don't forget to enjoy your awesome life.'

INTERPRETING EIGHT

VIRTUES

Vital, charged, alive, fearless, energised, vigorous, full of zeal, life of the party, powerful, inspired, healing, sustainable, solvent

VICES

Burned out, in debt, addicted to adrenaline, hesitant, an overachiever, fearful, drained, exhausted, anxious, unprepared

MOTTOS

'I am vital.'

'I am energised.'

'I am alive. I thrive!'

'I am strong. I am prepared. I am ready.'

FAMOUS EIGHTS

Mohammed Ali, Elvis Presley, Mother Teresa, Stephen Hawking, Serena Williams, Danny DeVito, Miles Davis

LIMITLESS — PSYCHIC — ACUITY — GRACEFUL
SOPHISTICATED — ELEGANT — ABSTRACT

IX

The number 9 is the master of all systems.

It is the most graceful, refined, sophisticated, mysterious and attuned of all the numbers.

It represents the 'subtle body': the invisible part of ourselves that can extend out to everything else. It is a remarkably powerful and sensitive number.

COLOUR	Purple
PLANET	Moon
SEPHIRAH	Yesod
DEFINITION	Foundation
YOGIC BODY	Subtle body
CATCHPHRASE	'Smooth operator' 'Mastery or mystery'

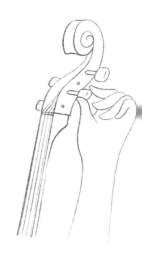

NINE IN ACTION

This is the number of grace, sophistication, elegance, refinement, and sublime intelligence. It has a level of intelligence that goes beyond the logic of the mind, and the ability to figure anything out. Whereas the number 3 offers wonderful brain power that, when harnessed appropriately, can tap into divine intelligence, the number 9 just has an almost mysterious sense of knowing that comes through sensitivity. It has the ability to permeate consciousness into realms that are unseen.

It is the number of subtlety. It is represented by the colour purple, and its planet is the moon. It is our inner selves: our subconscious. Our subconscious is very sensitive and hidden, but is aware of many signals and realities. It can hear and remember. Think of the phrase 'It's buried in the subconscious.' Yesod is the filter. Your subconscious mind picks up on every little thing. Keep it clear, and more will come through. The Moon is a sensitive energy field. Many traditions say that we draw on the Moon for our psychic internal knowing. The Moon is our internal selves and it's our hidden selves. The number 9 sees that which is unseen and that which is hidden. The catchphrase for 9 is 'Mastery or mystery'. Are you operating in your mastery? Or are you allowing this subtle energy to be too confusing and mysterious?

The number 9 is a very psychic number. When we're in touch with our subtle form, we're able to manoeuvre effortlessly and limitlessly through any situation. Our subtlety is what gives us the ability to master all systems. What does this mean? It means that we are able to let go of and project a part of our consciousness into anything, and that we're able to attain and assess information that isn't normally seen. The number 9 represents this graceful ability. It perceives everything. When you use the energy of 9 with grace and sophistication, so much will open up to you. This is what psychic ability is. When you're open, things will just come to you. It is a very intuitive number, but it also the heart of where real intuition lies, which is much more of a sophisticated science. When we allow our consciousness and grace to be still, we can achieve many miracles.

Those with strong 9s have a sophisticated intelligence suitable for working in many fields. I have had a lot of clients with significant 9s in their numerology chart that are doctors. What do doctors do? They diagnose and assess information that isn't necessarily readily available to the untrained eye. I've also worked with an acupuncturist. She could take my pulse and be able to tell if I had eaten something I wouldn't normally eat. To me, it seemed like a psychic power. It's also common for psychics and readers to have strong 9s in their numerology chart. With the ability to see the unseen, you can formulate a clear message out of the information you receive. On another level, strong 9s can also be seen in a person who works as an administrative assistant, or perhaps in IT – someone who can go into any corporation, company or consulting situation because they have the ability to figure out any system.

If you feel like you need to get a little sophisticated, work on your movement. My old Magick teacher had me learn the Alexander Technique and ballet to help me understand the relationship between sensitivity and strength in movement. Think of the level of mastery and purity that professional ballerinas demonstrate. Now, that takes a tremendous amount of strength and power. It requires great physical effort and endurance, but is performed with so much grace and sophistication that it actually looks like they're just floating around. Sensitivity gives you great strength.

This number gives you the power of limitlessness and the ability to manoeuvre through walls, time, space and different dimensions. It is not restricted to three dimensions. It's a very abstract and mystical number. There's a Magickal teaching that says, 'To understand the mysteries, one must be mysterious.' So own this energy field: embrace it, and the mystery of the universe. With the number 9, you're not limited to anything. You can't be confined. You can hear things a mile away. You can figure something out just like that. Our brains work more slowly than the speed of the universe and God. There's a teaching in Magick that says, 'You are slow, the universe is fast.' If you find yourself just getting a sense of something right away – an immediate, intuitive knowing – don't diminish or doubt it. The number 9 will know something right away, so use your intuition, don't censor it. This is true regardless of whether or not the number 9 applies to your personal numerology chart. The first thing that comes to you is almost always the right answer. Start to practise and play around with that idea. You shouldn't feel frantic. Be graceful, intuitive, correct, accurate and a master of all systems. The subtle body can cause intense sensitivities in everything.

NINE IN REFLECTION

The negative side of 9 is being so sensitive to what you're seeing or feeling that it puts you totally out of sorts because you can see the smallest faults or potential problems in any situation.

Everything is louder, brighter and perceivably more intense with the number 9. Try not to blow everything out of proportion. This can easily manifest as 'Princess and the Pea' syndrome.

Even smells can be more intense. I always joke that my mother is a 9 soul and she drives me crazy with the things she says she can smell. I swear, she'll still be able to smell something from a year ago. But all joking aside, the number 9 can give one tremendous ability and sensitivity to all of the senses. I can smell things in people's auras. It's not just a biological smell sensed through my nose. There's a psychic smell, too. When someone is a master of something, they do it with ease. I know a Chinese medicine healer who told me that they're able to smell certain ailments and conditions in their clients. To harness this in a positive way, always try to use this number for development, empowerment and prosperity.

Another potential negative side of the refined and graceful number 9 is the risk of being incredibly fragile. This is where we need to use all the numbers to make sure our bodies are empowered, and our minds are right and clear. A further negative side can be when mystery turns into confusion and unknowing. This number can be so overly sensitive that it turns mountains into molehills.

Can you sometimes be ungraceful? Are you ever crass? Are you rude? Are you a loud mouth? Are you rough around the edges? Is your head in the clouds? Do you have no sense of time or reality? It can go to that extreme.

It's important to stay grounded and steady with this energy field. Use your sensitivity as a power and a gift – don't allow it to overwhelm you. With practice, you will get better at this and become more attuned. But it's anything that's highly attuned and has a very high-frequency vibration. Now, honestly, that doesn't mean it's better than a lower-frequency vibration. It's simply how we manoeuvre and operate.

LESSONS FROM NINE

This number brings a wonderful ability for abstract thinking, and for seeing that which is unseen and that which might be hidden. It is the number of psychic abilities and high intuition. Often, people that are psychic aren't necessarily aware of their ability. It's just about being attuned to clues that other people may not be aware of, and this is something anybody can learn.

It's like a tracker's ability to track an animal. They will see and recognise things that the untrained eye would never notice: maybe footprints, or a broken twig, or a piece of gravel that's been moved in a slightly different way. The number 9 is a great number for detective work.

This number is called the 'master of all systems'. It has a sense of knowing. If you take subtle energy, spirits exist in subtle realms. They don't manifest in the heavier three-dimensional world that we live in, but our consciousness can expand to many different dimensions and ideas.

This number can really see a pattern. If you have a lot of 9s in your chart, it's good to be empowered, but not neurotically sensitive. This is a very strong number because it's limitless. That subtle invisible body can't be captured or taken down. Use it as a superpower. Even if you don't have a 9 in your chart, the number is accessible to you.

The planet of number 9 is the moon, which represents your deepest inner self. It's a little more mysterious. The number 9 is the number of the mystic. The mystic can unify everything, and sees how it's all one, so you can go into a higher consciousness in the 9 energy field.

The number 9 is very intricate. It's a more complex system and that's why it needs lighter, more refined energy to move through it. I call 9 the 'spiritual ballerina' because it has a very sophisticated, subtle and graceful energy field. It has a very intuitive and intelligent energy, and can manoeuvre into any space or realm. It's very multidimensional. It's not bound by walls. It can't be described. It can't be seen. The 9 energy field sees invisible realms far beyond what is here.

How can you elevate your 9? Start to look at your movements and speech. How graceful are you in your life? What are your movements like? Do you have refined tastes? If you want to improve these areas of your life, start doing everything with a level of mastery, grace and sophistication.

Often you can read books and gain wisdom through osmosis. I have a library of Magickal books, and there's an energy around it that goes into your psyche. You can pick up on it. The number 9 will read auras. It will sense anything. It can read minds. It's as if it has little antennas that can see, feel, understand and know.

If you keep seeing the number 9, the universe might be trying to tell you to get out of your box and limited viewpoint.

Where are you too confined?

Where are you getting lost or too spaced out?

Maybe it's a sign to be more sophisticated and graceful.

Where do you need to be more mysterious?

Maybe the universe is telling you that you are in a position of mastery and excellence.

INTERPRETING NINE

VIRTUES

Subtle, sophisticated, graceful, masterful, reflective, receptive, elegant, effortless, transcendent, sublime

VICES

Overly complicated, overly sensitive, neurotic, clumsy, spaced out, lost, despairing, obsessive, over-reactive, fragile, ungrounded, crass

MOTTOS

'I can figure it out.'

'Success is easy and effortless.'

'I'm a smooth operator.'

'I am limitless.'

FAMOUS NINES

Carl Jung, Mikhail Baryshnikov, Alice Coltrane, Jimi Hendrix, Quentin Tarantino, Jimmy Page, Lewis Carroll, John Lennon

STAR POWER — RADIANT — UNIQUE — NOBLE
MAJESTIC — GREAT — BRIGHT

10 is the number of radiance, nobility, royalty and greatness. It is all or nothing. It represents our largest, most dynamic, most powerful selves, which have the ability to always stand in dignity and humility.

COLOUR	Citrine, black, olive green, oxblood
PLANET	Earth
SEPHIRAH	Malkuth
DEFINITION	Kingdom
YOGIC BODY	Radiant body
CATCHPHRASE	'All or nothing'

TEN IN ACTION

The number 10 is spiritual nobility. On the Tree of Life, 10 is Malkuth, which means 'kingdom'. It is attributed to planet Earth, and its colours are earth tones (citrine, black, olive green and oxblood). We are spiritually noble people living in the kingdom of Earth.

The number 10 is large and in charge: it is always going to be seen. It has the radiance and warmth of the Sun. It is the energy that is always giving its light. It's about standing in that nobility, greatness and power.

There is a teaching that says, 'Prosperity comes from radiance', so let yourself shine. Let yourself be seen. This is the energy of a public figure. Regardless of whether they're well-known, no matter what level they're at, someone with the energy of 10 is always a star. Just think about your favourite coffee shop. Chances are, there's a barista that's the star of the show. This energy can be found in any type of business, any situation, any group of friends. There are always those types of people that carry themselves with a certain poise and regal quality – that is number 10. This number just lets it shine.

This is also called the number of 'all or nothing'. So, are you a number one or are you a zero? Number 10 energy, when it's homed in on in the right way, lets us know we should be doing great things that we will be seen and known for in the world. The downside of that, because this number is all or nothing, is that we might end up lying in bed, thinking, 'I should be doing something great in the world, but I'm such a worthless failure I can't even get up.' This is something that really has to be reconciled.

If you look at Lady Gaga's numerology, she's a double 10 and I think we all know just how famous and influential she is. It's important to understand that the energy of 10 should always stand in a humble righteousness. This number gives you the ability to recognise your true talents and stop hiding. I often see people who have strong 10s in their charts, but the energy is manifested as weakness –they should be doing something on a bigger stage, with a bigger platform, yet they're hiding behind their lightness and greatness. There's a prayer that says: 'I agree to be great; I surrender to the greatness of God.'

The number 10 can be a number of excellence. There is a greatness and spiritual nobility that comes with really standing in your own radiance and confidence. Where can you have more dignity in your life? Where could you go bigger? Where could you let yourself be seen? Where could you be more of a star?

This number is radiance. Where are you shining? How radiant are you? How empowered are you? It's the number of great empowerment. Treat yourself with the respect of nobility and treat others in the same way. You will see this radiance will bring a lot of prosperity to your life. Push yourself out there a little bit. Don't worry about getting criticised or ridiculed. You're not going to hurt anybody. The 10 energy needs to be seen – just own it. The world wants your radiance. The 10 energy is like walking into a room with your own entrance music as if you're a pro wrestler, or the main character in a film: there's a beautiful confidence.

It's that real rock star/movie star energy field, in the most elevated way. It is fame and visibility. Interestingly, it's actually the number that's most often connected to hair. To be honest, that's one of the reasons I have long hair. It is a very visible number with an extroverted energy.

Number 10 is fame and visibility. If you are talking about bricks and mortar, it's 'location, location, location'. You need your business to be seen and visible, whether it's a storefront or whether it's solely online.

We all have 10 energy. We're all made of the same substance as stars. When we stand in that noble radiance, we allow everyone else to shine, too, and it's actually a very humble place. With the energy of 10, we can use the number 0 to let go of our egos and our fears. I'm always amazed by how many people I do readings for that have 10s in their charts, but they are afraid to lean into it and step up for fear of being persecuted. This fear of being criticised could come from a past life or childhood trauma. But with 10, we're number one. We've moved past all our bullshit, and we're freakin' awesome. A good mantra for number 10 is: 'Even though I'm totally awesome, I still love and accept myself', because sometimes it's hard to accept that we're really great. So, if you're feeling down on yourself, incorporate some 10 energy.

We're all awesome, and we're all radiant, and so much of our prosperity comes from our radiance. We all have a radiant body, so let's build it up, let's be great, let's be prosperous. We are beautiful, vibrant souls, helping others step into their radiance and spiritual nobility.

TEN IN REFLECTION

This number is ultimately about humility. You must have humility in order to accept who you are and where you're at. If someone with a 10 in their chart doesn't take the lead on that, they will go on thinking they're a failure.

The opposite of humility is having too much power or intensity, and shining too brightly. I'm sure you have come across people like this, who are completely abrasive, overbearing and too much to handle. Often those are people with a lot of 10 energy that's simply out of balance. The key here is to stand tall and stand bright with a regal glory everywhere you walk in your life.

One of the negative sides of number 10 energy can be the desire to hide. Thinking about it: where in your life are you hiding? Get out of bed, get out of your little cave and start sharing the talents that you have with the world. That's one of the biggest lessons the number 10 has to offer: share your greatness.

It's also important to remember that this is not about status. It's not about fame for the sake of fame. The number 10 is about holding a very exalted space of majesty, dignity and honour. Hold yourself to that standard. When you do that, you help change the world, and that's true nobility.

Behaving with real majesty connects you to the higher dignity of the universe, so step into that honour. Don't be afraid of yourself and what you can accomplish.

LESSONS FROM TEN

The number 10 has the energy of greatness, but it can also have the energy of failure or perceived failure. It's part of the number's 'all or nothing' energy field. It always makes me think of the Will Ferrell movie *Talladega Nights*. In the film, the main character is influenced as a child by the rhetoric of his deadbeat alcoholic dad, who always tells him, 'Boy, if you ain't first, you're last.' This is a really powerful lesson to learn about the number 10 because the negative side of thinking you always have to be in first place, is that if you don't do everything with that level of status and achievement, you feel that you've failed. If you aren't winning an Oscar, Grammy or Emmy, or being an A+ student, or getting a promotion at work, people with 10s in their charts may translate that to being a failure. They will often feel as if they should be doing something 'bigger and greater' with their lives.

It's important to strive for balance when facing this duality. Remember, not being in first place doesn't mean you're in worst place. As much as we may strive for status (in astrology, the tenth house is the house of career, recognition and status in the world), it's important to always stay humble in your pursuits.

If someone with 10 energy is at the top of their game, there is no fear of threat, and it's a very divine, alpha energy. A true alpha encourages and never fears another alpha. I think there's a lot of misconceptions around alpha identity, and it can be dangerous: people think it means that you're domineering and somehow rule through fear. The world is riddled with fake alphas, especially men. You can identify a fake alpha easily because if someone is really comfortable with themselves and doesn't fear any threat, they'll allow and encourage other people to thrive. If you feel really comfortable in yourself and in your own greatness, then you're really strong in your 10 energy. You don't fear any threat, and you're not trying to dominate others because you're so empowered that instead you encourage others to step up too.

If you keep seeing the number 10, the universe is telling you that you're amazing. You're great. Maybe it's a message that it's time to shine and put yourself out there.

Or perhaps you are having a lot of doubts and insecurities at the moment?

INTERPRETING TEN

VIRTUES

Large and in charge, self-assured, giving, admirable, honourable, influential, renowned, popular, prominent, prestigious, humble

VICES

Shy, arrogant, entitled, loud, proud, shame, afraid of ridicule and humiliation, abrasive, overbearing, insecure, egomaniacal, susceptible to delusions

MOTTOS

'I am a star.'

'I am radiant.'

'I am great.'

'Even though I'm totally awesome, I still love and accept myself.'

'I agree to be great.'

FAMOUS TENS

Lady Gaga, Judy Garland, Grace Jones, Malcolm X, Coco Chanel, Dolly Parton, Jacqueline 'Jackie O' Kennedy Onassis

VAST — ICONIC — EXPANSIVE — FLOWING — INFINITE
THE WHOLE SHEBANG

The number 11 is sound current. It is the number that contains all of the numbers, and thus, 11 contains the entire cosmos. It is the infinite universe. It can be a number of tremendous expansion.

COLOUR	Invisible
PLANET	Infinite cosmos
SEPHIRAH	Da'ath
DEFINITION	Knowledge
YOGIC BODY	Sound
CATCHPHRASE	'Infinity'

ELEVEN IN ACTION

From singing bowls to gongs to binaural beats, we can use sound to heal, alter and shift our consciousness. Sacred language is called 'sound currents' when the sound and vibration of a word is the actual vibration of whatever that word is. This is found in sacred ancient languages such as Sanskrit and Hebrew. The sound patterns unlock codes, open doorways and allow us to access subtle realms: the things we can feel and see.

Whether sound currents are made using mantra, sacred music, sound therapies or healing, the sound is also our voice. Our voices are the sound vibrations of the whole universe. It's important to remember there are sounds that are not heard. In the Age of Aquarius (the sign of Aquarius is the 11th house in astrology), 11 holds the space of all of the vibrational frequencies of the universe, and anything can be accomplished with sound. In other words, as we tap into these different vibrational frequencies of the universe, we really can do anything. Those are the basic principles of Hermetic Magick. The entire universe is a series and sequence of different vibrational frequencies, and when we align ourselves to different frequencies, aka sounds, we can attract. So much can be done with sound; ancient cultures have always known this. Mystics and magicians have been taught that the pyramids were built using sound. If we can build pyramids with the power of sound, which is a technology we will soon rediscover, then we can build anything in our lives with the power of sound.

One of the most accessible ways that we use sound is with our words. The things we say become manifest, so if you spend a lot of your time complaining about things, being 'super negative', you're going to create opportunities for negative things to happen. So many of us have said things like, 'Oh, I'll never meet anybody,' 'I'll be alone the rest of my life', or 'I'll never have a job that's fulfilling.' These words have a real impact, and if you have 11s in your numerology chart, that impact gets even stronger.

There's a wonderful practice where you try not to complain for 90 days. I tried it once, and I think I lasted about nine minutes. It's interesting to see how quick we are to complain about things. Maybe someone cuts you off while driving, or it's too cold out, or too hot, or it's humid, or you're tired. There are endless things to complain about. It's much better to compliment than complain.

There's a teaching that says some of the most successful actors and performers in the world are people who are in love with their own sound current. How do you use your own voice? You don't have to be a singer or musician to tap into sound current. What is the vibrational frequency that you're putting out into the universe?

Beyond what we do with our voices, or the music that we play, our energy is always expanding outward, and it's always permeating everything around us. We create this projection of our vibration, aka our sound current. In the Age of Aquarius, the sound current is the most powerful tool. When used appropriately, it gives us tremendous power. At MIT university, they have developed equipment strong and sensitive enough to record and replay participants' sound currents in inanimate objects.

Now let's start to expand on the idea of sound vibrations that are in motion and expanding outward. Whales communicate using a sound frequency that can go to one hundred miles: the trajectory of sounds just keeps on going.

This tells us that sound is expansive, as is the number 11. When we utilise the energy of 11, it starts putting things out into the world that can take on a life of their own. It's a really good number for investing and residual income. You put some money into something, and then over time it just builds up. So it can have a very positive ripple effect. It's also a great number to use when building something and putting it out into the world. For example, I'm sitting working on this book right now, but once this is all said and done, the energy of this book (my sound current) is going to be out in the world, and if I tap into the energy of 11, it will keep taking on a life of its own. When you tap into your sound, whether you are running a business or working on other projects and ideas, know that we use the number 11 to go bigger, to expand, to touch more of the world, and more of the universe. Allow the energy of 11 to work for you.

The number 11 is very much in flow and in a groove with the universe. It can build momentum, and is the number of infinite possibilities. The best thing you can do with the energy of 11 is put your foot down and set off. By taking action, things around you will start to align with your destiny. You don't always have to know which direction you're going in. I often speak to people with 11s in their numerology chart, and they find that whatever they do, things just start to work out. They might say, 'Oh, I wanted to get into this particular profession, and I started down that road and things started to open up for me. And then I sabotaged it, because I thought, well, I don't know, is this the thing that I want to do? Let me try something else.'

The energy of the number 11 wants to try a lot of things, but sometimes it's just about being open to possibilities. When you're tapped into the infinite and your infinite self, your intuition will be strong.

I have a few clients here in Hollywood who are writers. A lot of writers are really good examples of 11 energy because they have to say, 'I'm going to do some work here now, and then I'm going to just put it out into the universe. Then the universe will take it.' Let's say it's a script. The universe takes that writer's script, and things start to snowball. The right people get attached to it, and next thing you know, the movie is getting made, and will hopefully be seen and felt by millions of people, and the writer will receive their royalties. This is the momentum of the number 11.

Hermetic Magick says: 'everything is vibration.' One of the best things you can do is look at your personal sound current. These sound waves and vibrations start in one place and they just expand out. At some point, the three-dimensional sound waves dissipate, but this sound and vibration can keep going. The things that we say really become real. As I explained earlier, if you have 11s in your chart, you need to be extra careful with this. It's really a blessing, though, because we can speak many things into existence, and we can create a lot of our life through the things we say. Our words are very important. The Magickal teaching is that when you empower your words by saying you're going to do something and then actually do it, you're creating a flow and a trust with the universe. Over time, your word will become so empowered that anything you say can manifest and become real.

The number 11 is passively active. It's a real opening. Don't short-circuit your infinite possibilities. Keep your sound current strong: it's your vibration. Your sound current is your you. It's the essence of your vibrational frequency. As you fall in love with your sound current and lock into this greater flow, infinite possibilities will show up for you.

ELEVEN IN REFLECTION

It is important for people with 11s in their chart to have a strong sense of self so they aren't drowned out. Things germinate with the energy of 11. Plant a bunch of little seeds to grow into a beautiful garden that is your life. This is a lesson to take one microscopically small thing and watch how it expands.

For example, when it comes to investing, the number one rule is to diversify. Some things may take off, while others are more slow-moving. With an 11 path, you are capable of creating a lot of revenue streams. There is a natural hustle and flow to working several jobs. You can do a lot of different things. You don't have to fall into the mindset of doing or being one thing. That's a societal idea you can let go of.

It's good to consolidate but still diversify. A word of warning, though: those with 11s in their chart can risk spreading themselves too thinly. Be cautious of this if you find yourself never really seeing things through.

A negative side of the 11 energy can be expansion that's so easy that you just do a little something and it starts to take on a life of its own. This means it can become a very lazy energy field. The 11 energy can just coast along and go with the flow because things work out without any real intention and without causing any meaningful change.

All humanity is looking for authentic, true, spiritual experiences. It is one of the most important teachings of this new era. In this new time and frequency for the human race, we all have to use our vibrational frequencies, our number 11 sound currents, to help send a positive experience out into the world.

The other challenge of this number is that because it's the infinite, that means there are infinite possibilities. I often see people with strong 11s in their charts who are capable of doing pretty much anything, but they often become paralysed by the choices – they don't know what to do. I always teach that the worst decision with the number 11 is no decision. Those with this number in their charts have to learn to take action. As you take that action, and you incorporate the energy of 11 into everything in your life, eventually things that you should be doing (your destiny) will start to show up.

LESSONS FROM ELEVEN

This number can just be so vast and big and overwhelming that you don't even notice any changes you are causing or any effect you are having on the world. That's one of the things we need to learn about this number. When you really start utilising the energy of 11, you can use its momentum and expansion for the things that you're already doing, and also the things that you want to do.

It's good to know that this number can help you expand whatever you need to. If you think about the infinite flow of the universe, there's definitely an energy for expansion. This number expands outwards, and it can infinitely expand inwards. So what are you expanding? If you have 11s in your chart, those are going to be some of your lessons. It comes down to your vibrational frequency being in tune with the infinite. When you tap into that infinite frequency, anything is possible.

If you keep seeing the number 11, let the universe work for you a little more. It might be a sign that you're in a really powerful flow, and powerful growth is ahead.

Maybe it's a message to get out from under yourself.

Or perhaps it's time to stop complaining.

INTERPRETING ELEVEN

VIRTUES

Tremendous, polymathic, expansive, extraordinary, generative, incredible, acts as a conduit, diverse, initiates a snowball effect

VICES

Late blooming, inert, stifled, stunted, blocked, lacking in direction, caught in the undertow, stagnant, slow to start

MOTTOS

'Success flows to me and I flow to success.'

'I will get out of the way of the universe, and let the hand of God work for me.'

'I set things in motion.'

'I create with my words.'

FAMOUS ELEVENS

David Bowie, Oprah Winfrey, Leonardo DiCaprio, Madonna, Salvador Dalí, John F. Kennedy, Jennifer Aniston, Duke Ellington

FROM NOTHING CAME EVERYTHING — PRIMORDIAL EXISTENCE
SILENCE — BEGINNING OF CREATION

In the Magickal tradition, 0 is a number and a non-number. The primordial existence, on some level, comes out of nothing.

In Qabalah, we have the Ain, the Ain Soph, and the Ain Soph Aur.

Creation comes from nothing: Ain is nothing. Ain Soph is limitless. Ain Soph Aur is limitless light. This is the flow of creation.

SEPHIRAH	'Ain. Ain Soph. Ain Soph Aur'
DEFINITION	'Nothing. Limitless. The limitless light'
CATCHPHRASE	'Nonexistence to existence'

ZERO IN ACTION

This number is, and it isn't. It's a very mysterious number, a non-number. Think about that mystery for a moment. In the yogic tradition, 0 is the 'shuniya state', which is the state of absolute stillness, absolute purity and absolute connection to divinity, because there is zero separation. This is where time stops. There is no separation between the individual and divinity, between you and your soul, between you and creation. It's where everything, perhaps for one instantaneous moment, becomes absolved into the ecstasy of all existence. Some traditions call it Nirvana. Magick would call it 'being inflamed with spirit' or 'being inebriated with spirit'. This is the purest of zones, where you can lose track of your mind, of your ego, of everything that you think of as 'you', and exist as pure existence. Or should I say as pure non-existence? Which one is it?

This is a state in which you've completely absolved into something bigger, higher and greater. It's a state of pure stillness. When you're in that place of stillness, so much can transform for you. In the Magickal tradition, Hippocrates (the Aeon card in the Tarot) is the child, and represents a state of purity. His secret teaching is silence. It is said in this new Aeon of Horus and this new consciousness for humanity, silence is part of the sound current. When we are in this shuniya state, we go back to a primordial beginning.

In Tarot, the number 0 is the Fool. The Fool is considered the primordial zero point of all creation, as if everything comes out of this void. This number is absolute stillness. It is authenticity at a level that may transcend the psyche. The Fool is foolish because the Fool has no idea that something is not possible. This number has no limitations beyond any of the other numbers we discussed. The Fool gets very deep because the teachings of the Fool are actually that all of the cards come out of the Fool, come out of the zero state. At this zero point, we can create so much. Pay attention to your life when you can be still and when you can be silent. Imagine experiencing no thought.

In maths, the number 0 is really interesting. There's a teaching that says, 'However much money you're earning, add a zero.' Let's say you make £60,000 ($80,000) a year. Well, if you add a zero to it, now you're making £600,000 ($800,000). Add a zero to that, and you are making £6 million ($8 million) a year. Think about that interesting power dynamic. However, if you multiply any number by 0, its value diminishes significantly – to 0. The number 0 is this vortex and threshold. There is a spiritual teaching that says whatever it is you don't want in your life, you can multiply it by 0 to clear it out. This number is an opportunity for a reset and a fresh start, a clean slate.

In a numerology chart, 0 will only come up as a gift number every 100 years. For example, if you're reading this, those people born in the year 2000 will have this gift number. It is groundbreaking. When we enter a new century, we are entering a whole new streamline of consciousness, a ground zero. You will learn more about this on page 172, but a gift number of 0 means an innate talent of stillness and supreme wisdom, knowledge and existence. It can really get to the core, to the heart, to the essence of any matter. It transcends feeling. It transcends the mind. Its transcends the highest intuition. This number offers the very powerful gift of existing – or not existing – right in the moment. It's a very transcendental number.

ZERO IN REFLECTION

The negative side of this number would be non-existence, hiding, dissipating and having a harder time functioning in the world. But generally speaking, this number is a gift, bringing positive talents that come to you easily. It has the ability to transcend any limitations, any type of cultural identity or gender identity. There are no restrictions with the number 0.

LESSONS FROM ZERO

There's another deep teaching in Magick that also says: 'One equals zero, zero equals one.' That is not meant to be intellectually comprehended. Think of this number as a transcendental meditation, something that will expand your consciousness by getting rid of your consciousness.

The emphasis on the virtue of silence with 0 goes deep. Silently meditate on that and see what evolves in your life. When we get to that silence, it allows for a higher creation to come through.

On a practical note, look at how all of your chattering, gossiping, babbling, useless talking or complaining can sap your energy. I encourage you to be aware and mindful of your words.

This number will open up a lot of mysteries within you. This silence will open up a lot of mysteries within you. So take some time, be in that silence. Pay attention to your words. See how much your energy and your will are being dissipated, and make your words more empowered. Spend time daily in silence, to the best of your ability.

If you keep seeing the number 0, this is a message that maybe it's time to bring more stillness into your life. The universe could be asking you, what would you like to get rid of? Or what would you like to add?

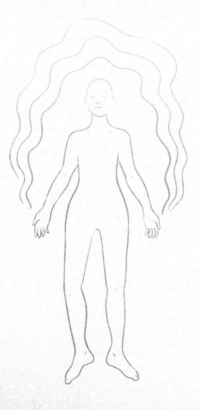

THE NUMEROLOGY CHART

With this system of numerology, which is based on Qabalistic tantric numerology, each person has a specific placement of numbers that is called their 'numerology chart'. Your numerology chart is based on your date of birth. Numerology is a very direct, simplified, streamlined and pure look into the essence of your soul, your talents and the work that needs to be done. It is important to understand the different placements and their meanings before diving into what a particular number means in each placement. Each one of these placements can serve as a reminder and a tool for your individual success.

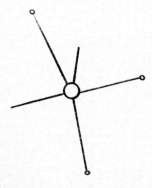

SOUL

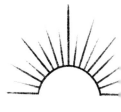

Your soul placement is the day you were born.

So if you were born on the 27th of the month, your soul is a 9 (2 + 7 = 9).

The soul placement in your numerology chart is the essence of who you are. It is the purest, most unadulterated, truest parts of you. The soul placement represents the area that you strive toward in your life. It is the number you are trying to come into in order to have a greater experience of its energy and essence. Simply put, your soul placement is you.

I'm sure you've heard the expression, 'That person has a lot of soul.' It is often used when talking about artists or musicians. Your soul can shine through, creatively, artistically and in many different ways. Your soul placement number gives you a hint of what this is for you. It shows you where you can find real fulfillment in your life. It's your happy place.

Your soul number is a frequency that you're working on and learning about. You may not always be there. You grow and evolve into this number. The soul number shows you your talents and strengths. These can translate to a career, hobbies and many other aspects of your life.

The soul takes some work. You are trying to utilise more and come into more. The soul can often be a marker of where you can go back to when you're not sure which direction to go in next.

It's important, though, to know that your soul is bigger than a number. The system of numerology and learning about the soul through your number is a really good starting point to help you get in touch with who you really are and where your true talents lie. What mission or motivation aligns with the destiny of your soul?

KARMA

Your karma placement is the month in which you were born.

So if you were born in December (12), reduce it down to 3 (1 + 2 = 3).

The karma placement in your numerology chart shows you what you were born to master and understand. Let go of the mindset that karma equals some kind of punishment or reward. Simply put, karma is about the lessons you are meant to learn in this lifetime.

Many spiritual traditions teach us that we are incarnated to learn lessons and burn off karma, and give us tools and practices to help us do just that. Numerology can be used as one of those practices. Armed with the knowledge of your karma number, you are given a good understanding of the assets you have and the deficiencies that you need to work on. It is important that you embrace this number and try not to run from it.

Think of it as a wonderful instruction manual that says, 'Pay attention to this area of your life. Work on these ideas and concepts. These are the areas in which you're meant to be more proficient.'

Get rid of the notion that karma is the universe conspiring against you to take you down and out. Think of karma more like cause and effect. Have you ever heard the phrase 'Karma's a bitch?' Well, karma is only a bitch when you don't put in the work. For example, if you're driving down the highway and your car suddenly runs out of fuel, that's the karma of not paying attention to your fuel gauge. Perhaps you were looking at the beautiful scenery, or getting lost in a podcast, or texting when you shouldn't have been – whatever caused it, the karma is getting stuck on the side of the road. The 'good karma' is noticing you need more fuel, pulling over to a petrol station and filling up your tank, which enables you to keep driving. That is your reward. Karma is in your hands.

GIFT

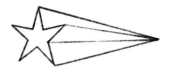

Your gift placement is calculated using the last two digits of the year in which you were born.

So if you were born in 1989, your gift number is 8 (8 + 9 = 17, then 1 + 7 = 8). Continue to add the numbers until you have either a single digit, or a 10 or 11.

The gift placement of your numerology chart reveals your divinely given talent. It's your superpower. This number tells you what you're good at. The best aspects of your gift number are easily accessible to you. You are efficient and skilled in this area, and it comes to you effortlessly. The key to this talent is recognising you have it in the first place. It's very common to take your talents for granted, treating them as a normal, everyday occurrence – because, for you, that's what they seem like.

We are often unaware of our gifts. So it is important to recognise your gifts and talents. Sometimes you're given a gift, and it's up to you to unwrap it and start using it. Be conscious of your gift and apply it to your life. There are many ways for your gift to show itself in the world, whether it's in art, science, intelligence, design, healing, communication, friendships, bowling, patting your head and rubbing your belly while standing on one leg and chewing gum ... the possibilities are endless. It's wise to remember that not only is this your gift, it's also your gift to give to the world. The world wants and needs your special superpower. Share it!

There's a teaching that says: 'There's a way through any block.' If you're ever feeling stuck or unsure of how to navigate a situation in your life, remember your gift. Apply it and use it for greater success.

When you are aware of and comfortable with your gifts, you can enter any situation with more capacity, ability, knowledge and trust in your real skills and talents. This is the thing that you can really gift and give to the world. It's yours to give freely.

EXPERIENCE

Your experience placement is calculated using the 4 digits of the year in which you were born.

So If you were born in 1989, you have an experience of 9
(1 + 9 + 8 + 9 = 27, then 2 + 7 = 9). Continue to add the number until
you have either a single digit, or a 10 or 11.

The experience placement of your numerology chart is the number you have developed a working relationship with over many lifetimes. You have a lot of knowledge and expertise in the concepts and teachings revealed by this number.

You should have an understanding of and experience in all the facets of this number's energy field, but don't assume that all the assets of the number will come to you. It is possible that you may have lifetimes of experience in the deficient side of the number. This might be something that keeps coming up for you.

Having a particular number in your chart doesn't always mean you access or utilise the virtuous side of the number. Whatever the number is, you should always move towards its positive, vital tendency. You should have a full understanding of the negative and positive sides of the number, and through lifetimes of experience, you will know how to use it for good, however that may show up for you in your life.

Whereas the gift placement comes to us quite miraculously, the experience placement is a number that we have developed a relationship with time and time again. These are energy fields and talents that manifest in many different possibilities. This is what we've spent lifetimes working with, and there is a comfort zone in this energy field. Think about those people that are gifted musical prodigies by the age of 9. Then think about those who are equally talented and put in the work through practice and dedication.

LIFE PATH

Your life path number is your entire birthday, added one single digit at a time, then reduced down to a single digit, or a 10 or 11.

For example, if your birthday is 28 March 1986, your life path number is 10 (2 + 8 + 3 + 1 + 9 + 8 + 6 = 37, and 3 + 7 = 10).

The life path placement in your numerology chart is the path you walk down to get to the fulfillment of your soul. This is your journey: your mission in life. It's your call to action, what you need to be doing with your life. It may be easy, or you might find it challenging. This is your go-to. This is your compass. This is the number that guides you to your destination.

You use your path to get to your soul. The soul is what we want to be experiencing. The path is our mission, and work, and what we should be doing to get to where we need to go. It's where you have to take action. It helps you navigate and gives you direction. It is your overall frequency and mission.

You can learn a lot from assessing your soul and life path numbers. They can show you things like what you might be good at in a career. But, of course, everything is bigger than this. There is far more to existence than what we do to earn money.

You may overhear people say, 'I'm a 3' or 'I'm a 9'. Often when they say this, they're referring to their life path number. This is the number of your entire birthday: your overall number.

Imagine you are walking in the forest and you get lost. You come across several paths, but there's only one you should go down.

Your life path is the path you are meant to take in life. It is a good guide to your destiny or purpose. It's not that it comes easily: sometimes it's challenging. But the path is what you need to be doing. It may not always be what you think you're interested in or passionate about. This is a very significant number to utilise in your life.

Think of it like driving down the road. There might be traffic. You might get pulled over for speeding. You might run out of fuel because of your horrible karma. Sometimes you might be cruising down the motorway, jamming to your favourite songs, one tune after another, feeling like you're in the zone. At other times, the car might break down. You might get a flat tyre. There could be detours. You might decide to pull over to check out a beautiful view or smell the flowers by the side of the road. You might stop for ice cream. In our world of 'destiny seekers', it's good to learn that destiny is a state of being. It doesn't end. It's the path and the journey you take.

This path has your name on it. Follow it. When you use your life path number, you can navigate any situation in your life. You can handle whatever comes up and whatever obstacles are thrown at you. If you stay consistent and true to your path, moving steadily into your destiny, you will succeed.

The life path number is action-orientated. You may not have any awareness or experience of this number. On one level it's within you, but on another level it's outside of you because you have to move in that direction.

The placement of your life path number can help you to understand your mission and purpose in life. Whenever it seems as if all is lost, look at your life path number and it will tell you where you need to go. It will allow you to get centred. Stay true. This is your mission. Just do it.

HOW TO CREATE A CHART

A numerology chart has five placements: soul, karma, gift, experience and life path. Your individual chart is based on your birthday. In this system we reduce all numbers down to a single digit, unless we arrive at the number 10 or 11. Here is an example of a birth date we're going to use to create a basic numerology chart.

10TH AUGUST 1983

PLACEMENT	NUMBER
SOUL Calculated based on the day on which you were born.	**=10** Because we arrived at 10, we keep as 10.
KARMA Calculated based on the month in which you were born.	**=8** In this example it's August, the eighth month of the calendar year.
GIFT Calculated based on the last two digits of the year you were born.	**=11** 83 becomes 8 + 3 = 11.
EXPERIENCE Calculated based on the four digits of the year in which you were born.	**=3** 1 + 9 + 8 + 3 = 21, which becomes 2 + 1 = 3
LIFE PATH Calculated based on your entire birth date (day, month and four-digit year).	**=3** 8/10/1983 becomes 8 + 1 + 0 + 1 + 9 + 8 + 3 = 30 which becomes 3 + 0 = 3

See? It's an easy, simple addition. That's it. That's a whole numerology chart. Now we turn to the art of interpretation.

Note: Remember that different countries reverse the month and day when writing dates, so the date above could be written as 10/8/83 in the UK, but 8/10/83 in the US. If you're working with a date given in this format, make sure you know which number is the day and which is the month.

Interpreting a numerology chart

As I give brief descriptions of the different numbers in different placements, it's really important to remember that you should use this information as a catalyst to open up your own consciousness and wisdom.

Try to think of these numbers as spiritual concepts, teachings and symbols of different energetic frequencies. Someone's personal numerology chart will show tendencies that they have access to. It is wise to remember that no matter what your numerology chart contains, you can still utilise all of these numbers and their teachings. The numbers shown in your chart are simply the talents you have access to, things to be mindful of and tendencies you might lean towards. Every single person is different, and these energies and numbers come through in slightly different ways with slightly different variations depending on the specific reading. It is unique to the person.

Some people may have too strong a relationship with the numbers, causing them to get stunted, or limit the effectiveness of their readings. In my experience, it is important that you don't put your own personal thoughts, personality and agenda into the reading. You have to open up to something higher, and let it come through you. This process opens you up. You will start to develop a stronger relationship with your higher consciousness.

The descriptions are meant to give you a little insight and some clues, but, as with any type of divination, it's about opening up your intuition. Let these numbers speak to you. I often recommend that you imagine you're a child telling a story. Let go of your mind. Let go of your ego, which will always censor itself. Tune into your intuitive responses, which are generally instantaneous. Go with that answer. You don't have to be born with 'special gifts' or 'psychic powers' in order to do this. It's like any other art form, practice or discipline: the more you do it, the better you get. So relax into it. Allow it to be fun and enjoyable. You're simple telling a story about your soul.

SOUL OF 1

If you have a soul number of 1, you are someone that should always stay connected to the creator. This number can be very artistic, with an energy of consolidated focus. It suggests someone who is in alignment with their soul. With this placement, your soul is at the highest level of fulfillment. Go out there and co-create with God. This number is the energy of creation, co-creation and connection.

With a soul number of 1, you have the number of the soul in the soul placement. This gives you a tremendous ability to get into the zone of what you're doing. Don't overthink it. It is rare and auspicious. You have direct access to a higher experience and tremendous ability to co-create with the universe. Your happy place is to follow your heart.

KARMA OF 1

A karma number of 1 means you need to work on connecting with your soul. You need to know it's okay to follow your heart and not overthink your way out of the life you really want. Remember, the number 1 is about 'heart over head'. One of the biggest life lessons of a 1 karma placement is to follow your heart instead of your head. Are you out thinking your way out of a wonderful life? Are you applying too much intellect? Or are you going nowhere over those deep, satisfying feelings of the heart? The lessons here are about living in and creating a life full of soul satisfaction. Now remember, this can also take another trajectory. The extreme opposite of this is someone who only follows their heart without thinking about it. This will lead to them never accomplishing anything because they're just following every single whim or fancy. It is important to keep this in balance, but remember the key is mastering the heart.

GIFT OF 1

A gift number of 1 means you can easily access the essence of your soul. In other words, you got soul. You can easily get in the zone and get into the flow. You have an innate understanding of both the head and the heart. You have easy access to who you really are. Your head says, 'I think I know who I am', and your heart says, 'I feel who I am.' You have a natural ability to co-create with the universe. Someone with a gift of 1 has natural artistic talents, but you can be an artist of many things: painting, music, writing, athletics, business, accounting, etc. As ever, these numbers can manifest themselves in different ways. The gift of 1 shows someone with the ability to bring that essence into everything they do. Simply put – your talent is staying in the groove. Use your gifts wisely.

EXPERIENCE OF 1

If you have an experience placement of 1, you may have spent many lifetimes as an artist or a creator and a divine conduit. An experience of 1 means you can easily access the fulfillment of your heart and soul, and your life's mission. You have the ability to clear out any illusions that serve no purpose in the truth and honesty of your incarnation.

LIFE PATH OF 1

Go down the road where you are always in touch with your soul. You are always co-creating. You are meant to have a life of depth and soul fulfillment.

SOUL OF 2

If you have a soul number of 2, you are someone who is very open and loving. The highest aspect of 2 is concerned with beautiful, lovely things, like community, family, romantic partnerships, work environments and parenting. In the soul placement, 2 is very inclusive and loves to love. A soul of 2 means you are going to be open to possibilities and able to reach a wonderful, fluid, adaptive state. When used appropriately, this number is a receptive, open space. This number gives you the intuitive sense and wisdom to know what truly fulfills you. When you are content in this space, you are not looking for the outside to fill some void within you. A soul placement of 2 helps you say yes to the right things. The highest energy of the 2 soul is that you're connected to your own divinity and you are an open conduit of that, meaning you can make and receive the connections that you want.

KARMA OF 2

A karma of 2 will often take on the 'longing to belong' part of this number. The deficient aspect of the 2 vibration is too much wanting and too much longing for fulfillment. True fulfillment comes from divinity, from the experience of your soul. If you have a karma placement of 2, be mindful of what it is that you're trying to fill yourself with. Since 2 wants to fill itself so badly, it's key lesson to master is discernment. What is it that you're falling in love with?

As the number 2 is about the open space, ask yourself how open you are. The deficient side of this number could involve being too trusting, and free-flowing. It's good to be open-minded, but you also need to be reasonable. A karma of 2 can leave you with a classic case of FOMO (fear of missing out).

You may find yourself always searching for approval from others.

If you have a karma of 2, don't let your romantic relationships be the be-all and end-all. Those with this number must learn about real fulfillment, which can ultimately only be reached through divinity and your soul.

GIFT OF 2

If you have gift placement of 2, you may find you can very easily make connections. The gift of 2 can receive anything that it wants and it can make quick and immediate connections with others that can bring about bigger and greater opportunities. Someone with a gift of 2 will be able to read others easily and intuitively.

On a deeper level, 2 is connected with the wisdom of the universe. It's your highest identity before God. It's you. When used correctly, this number has an intuitive sense of purpose. Someone with a gift of 2 knows when to say yes and what they don't want. They have a great gut instinct.

EXPERIENCE OF 2

If you have an experience placement of 2, you have been working with this number for many lifetimes. If you've been working with the strong side of it, you have made the right connections. You're able to attract very positive, very harmonious and very righteous relationships in your life. If you have experience with the deficiency side of 2, that means you're still working on it. In general, an experience of 2 means you know how to make the right connections and receive what you want.

LIFE PATH OF 2

Someone with a life path of 2 needs to say yes, to be intuitive and open to possibilities. A life path of 2 means always knowing that you're super secure, fulfilled by your soul and your own divinity. Stay open to possibilities and let divinity intuitively guide you.

SOUL OF 3

Someone with a soul placement of 3 has access to a lot of power and confidence. It is someone who has the potential and ability to be a courageous, natural leader. If this is your soul number, your happy place is when you are a natural boss and power player in the world. Someone with a soul of 3 is an entrepreneur, someone who can really start and run their own operation, a builder and achiever. Build it and something will grow. Life is good. The optimism of this number can change your frequency, which helps create a lot of success.

KARMA OF 3

Someone with a karma placement of 3 generally needs to work on their courage, confidence and strength. They may be someone who is supposed to learn how to be a stronger leader in their life, and just needs the courage to do it. The number 3 represents the positive mind, which can lead to way too much thinking. This tendency to analyse every single detail or situation can lead to 'analysis paralysis', where you struggle to actually take action. Someone with a karma of 3 can either be inactive or overactive, never taking the time to utilise their intuition.

This is a very accurate number. Remember: the devil is in the details. When you get bogged down in the details, you can lose sight of the bigger picture. This number can have workaholic tendencies. It can be overly focused, and fail to leave room for abstract thinking and joy. If you have a karma of 3, you're learning how to come into your self-empowerment and courage. This is a self-starter energy. Someone with a karma of 3 may be too bossy, too rigid and too stiff, to the extent that they become uncreative. We are always working in balance with these numbers. Learn to take action by reaching a balance between analysing with intellect and going with your gut instinct.

GIFT OF 3

Someone with a gift placement of 3 has easy access to their courage, strength, power, stamina, righteousness, leadership, brilliance, intelligence and entrepreneurial skills. This number is a go-getter. Use your gifts wisely.

EXPERIENCE OF 3

An experience placement of 3 can go in either direction, but generally speaking, someone with this experience placement is going to be comfortable standing in power and authority. You have probably spent lifetimes in some sort of position of leadership, whether in politics, business or society, so use this experience to give you the courage to lead and guide others. Be mindful, though, of being too extreme, too courageous and too assertive.

LIFE PATH OF 3

It is encouraged that someone with a life path of 3 get into a position of authority or power: to run a company, activate their entrepreneurial spirits, build a business or start a foundation. Remember, the life path is the direction you should take in life. The number 3 is the power centre, the commander-in-chief. If your life path placement is a 3, step into this role. It's all about having the courage and optimism to build the foundation from which your dreams can grow.

SOUL OF 4

Someone with a soul placement of 4 is generally very open-minded, accepting, loving and compassionate. They have the ability to stay in the neutral mind to access truth and reality and not take it personally. This number is not moved by logic or emotion: it is reality. It is life on life's own terms. Someone with a soul of 4 doesn't judge others and understands that every individual is going through their own spiritual growth on their own journey. This is a 'love thy neighbour' energy. It's important to have self-acceptance. The very highest state of a soul of 4 is staying in the bliss of the moment, with no troubles from the past and no anxiety about the future. When the soul of 4 is in that state, all the possibilities will come to you.

KARMA OF 4

A karma placement of 4 may often take the negative tendency, which can lead to the person being very resentful, very closed off and very judgmental. They may be critical of others and very critical and self-punishing of themselves. Someone with a karma of 4 can also be too passive and enabling, failing to set any boundaries. They may let too much slide. People with this karma placement need to learn to forgive the past. The number 4 is in the word 'forgive'. Those with a karma of 4 need be in the moment, forget about the past, and let go of their anxiety, fear and judgement about the future. Be here now. There's nothing like the gift of the present.

GIFT OF 4

Someone with a gift placement of 4 has the natural ability to accept others, be very open-minded, say yes to many possibilities and hold the frequency where many options will come to them. Think about the four corners of the world. Due to the neutral nature of the number 4, this gift placement enables you to assess the truth of every single situation and open up without discrimination. If you have this gift placement, you will be able to hear all sides of a story and will intuitively know how to make the right decision. The key word here is open-mindedness. Use your gifts wisely. When tapped into a true, pure, in-the-moment heart space, you can accept you're exactly where you need to be. You can let go of the fear and anxiety, and use the heart frequency to open up a lot of miracles and allow them to come to you.

EXPERIENCE OF 4

Someone with an experience placement of 4 is able to utilise their talents of open-mindedness and ease of fluid possibility. This experience placement can enable you to really tap into the energy of the heart and love the world in a much higher way. Someone with an experience of 4 has spent many lifetimes giving compassion to the world.

LIFE PATH OF 4

If you have a life path placement of 4, you are somebody who is of service to the world through humanitarian and charitable acts. The number 4 is fair, righteous and loving. If you have this life path placement, you will find that your calling is to do things that can bring forth a loving harmony: to be open to the truth, listen to the truth and bring that into every aspect of the world. We live in a world that desperately needs more love, acceptance and forgiveness. Help lead the way.

SOUL OF 5

Someone with a soul placement of 5 is a natural teacher and communicator. They feel grounded in their body and know how to take action. The number 5 is a natural editor and corrector, and someone with a soul of 5 stands up for themselves. The negative side of this soul number might be a tendency to be vindictive or lacking in motivation. When you are using the number 5 correctly, you're able to communicate your needs to yourself and others. You're also able to use the physical body in more powerful ways. It's about force and assertion.

KARMA OF 5

A karma placement of 5 often implies that a person may need to focus a lot of attention on developing their relationship with power and the physical body. Sometimes people with this placement do not know how to communicate, apply boundaries or say no. It's important for someone with a karma of 5 to understand that assertion is not aggression. If they do not learn how to assert and communicate what they want, they may harbour resentment. Assertion, power, correction, balance and utilising the physical body are all tools that can help with mastering this number. Coming into the energy of a teacher and a communicator will clear and open up so many of these challenging patterns. Since the number 5 is so explosive and powerful, a little goes a long way. Always keep moving, and a greater shift can move you towards your rightful destiny.

GIFT OF 5

Someone with a gift placement of 5 is naturally empowered, has an instinctual sense of what they want and feels confident going after it. They are often a natural teacher, communicator and guide to others. Even though it's your gift number, it's always important to know that with a 5 energy, you need to apply follow-through. Use your gifts wisely.

EXPERIENCE OF 5

If you have an experience placement of 5, you are someone who has spent lifetimes as a teacher, guide or editor. Working with the number 5, you should have a good sense of who you are and what you want. Someone with an experience of 5 will find that communicating, setting an example and being a leader who people turn to for guidance will come very naturally for you. This number gets to the point. You'll find that exercise and physicality will bring you a lot of joy and can be very much a great 'go-to' therapy. The 5 energy comes in, correcting wrongs and eliminating problems. Use the forces of 5 for good.

LIFE PATH OF 5

If you have a life path placement of 5, your path to fulfillment is in a position of leadership and guiding others. Your life path empowers you to assert yourself in order to effect change and correct, improve and balance all situations. The number 5 strives for justice as its highest virtue. This number is all about communication. Someone with this life path placement might be a public speaker, publisher, video editor or prosecutor. The number 5 loves exercise and body movement, so this life path placement could also mean you are a dancer, weightlifter, yogi, etc. Be an example. Be a leader. Be a guide. The sculpture already exists within the stone: all you have to do is chisel away the parts that aren't needed. Go after it.

SOUL OF 6

If your soul placement is 6, you strive for a holy and reverent life. This number brings divinity to every situation. You naturally bring a harmony and sacredness to your spaces. The number 6 is very orderly. It is the beauty of the cosmos. It is dedicated to spiritual development and self-improvement. It is a very committed, devoted and dedicated energy field. Your happy place is a sacred space.

KARMA OF 6

If your karma placement is 6, you will need to master diligence, follow-through and consistency. This is the number of orbit and flow. The negative side of 6 can be getting stuck in a rut, where everything moves on autopilot without causing any effective change in the world ... or, more importantly, in your life. If you're ever feeling stuck, it's wise to remember that the number 6 has the ability to change its destiny. Your karma calls on you to do something every single day, and create things with divinity and purpose. This is your connection to something higher and greater than what is in front of you. Remember, Rome wasn't built in a day. Apply this teaching to your life. Make everything you're doing a little more sacred.

GIFT OF 6

If you have a gift placement of 6, you have a natural talent to create and hold highly energised sacred spaces that come in alignment with divinity and destiny. Cleanliness is godliness. You are someone who can effect change through prayer and meditation, and lead a very direct, open spiritual experience. You can make any situation come together to be more harmonious and peaceful. The key is to remember that you are the creator of sacred order. Use your gifts wisely.

EXPERIENCE OF 6

If you have an experience placement of 6, you have spent many lifetimes as a spiritual seeker and a spiritual practitioner. This number has a clear knowing and vision. It is attuned to the wisdom of mother nature, and holds a sense of reverence and ritual. The 6 energy field is often very devotional and dedicated to the evolution of the soul. Don't get bogged down in the small-vision, 'small town' frequency. Get into the right flow and zone of your higher evolution and purpose. Since you've spent so many lifetimes with your spiritual growth, you have focus and an inherent knowledge that your destiny is to produce change.

LIFE PATH OF 6

If your life path placement is 6, you are a harmoniser. This is a path of great spiritual growth and dedication. You are a natural networker, and can help others connect to their own destiny. The number 6 is an agent and ambassador. Whether you're a spiritual agent, Hollywood agent, literary agent or secret agent, you are the connector and the conduit. You are a representative, working for a higher cause. Someone with a life path of 6 has a greater ability to access the divine, and brings divinity into this realm and into all of the work they do. The sixth chakra is the third eye. It's an all-seeing, all-knowing, 'visionary' energy field. It opens up your destiny. As you are in touch with something higher, the life path of 6 means you have access to the big picture and the diligence and consistency to follow through. Stay centred.

SOUL OF 7

If you have a soul placement of 7, you're here to make the world a better and nicer place. Someone with a soul of 7 loves to elevate everything and everyone around them. You know how to beautify everything. Since 7 is the number of the aura and your natural habitat, when it is bright and prosperous, you want to help others be more prosperous. Someone with a soul of 7 has a security within themselves and can give back, like a little angel helping people. You are a natural emotional healer. What brings your soul true fulfillment is uplifting yourself and others. A 7 soul is a very sensitive, considerate and caring person.

KARMA OF 7

The energy of the number 7 likes to make things nicer for others, but the downside of that is losing track of your own needs and overextending yourself. You need to work on being strong enough in yourself, staying true to yourself and taking care of yourself first, so you are more empowered to help others. Your sensitivity is a strength, so it's important not to let the outside influence you so much. Someone with this karma placement might be extra sensitive to what they consume, whether that's food, other people's vibes or social media. It's important to keep your personal auric zone powerful and stand in your own security and confidence. Don't let other people's bad vibes affect you. With a karma of 7, you may easily feel unprotected, too vulnerable, and as if the world is a threat. It's important to be encouraging to yourself.

If your 7 energy is weak, everybody else's energy is going to rub off on you, and you'll find you are highly sensitive to all things that you consume. So if you have a karma of 7, it's really important to keep your aura vital and strong so that these things have much less of an effect on you. You can't always help everybody as much as you may want to, so it's your job to help yourself first, and stay in your vital, protective, nurturing zone.

GIFT OF 7

If you have a gift placement of 7, you elevate every situation just by being in it. You naturally bring a sweet, lovely, charming energy to the table. You uplift and encourage other people, and have a natural sense of artistic aesthetic and beauty. Someone with a gift of 7 knows how to use empathy and sensitivity to genuinely heal and help others. Use your gifts wisely.

EXPERIENCE OF 7

If you have an experience placement of 7, this means you've been working with the energy of elevation for lifetimes. You're good at making people feel good. You're good at holding space for others, whether that's by lending a helping hand, holding the door open, buying somebody a coffee, doing charitable deeds, etc. Your beautiful presence and exchanges have the power to uplift any room. It's the energy of an upgrade. Strong Venus energy has nice stuff, and the number 7 has an artistic sense of beauty and style.

LIFE PATH OF 7

If you have a life path placement of 7, it's your job to make the world a better place ... whatever that means to you. Someone with a life path of 7 might become a therapist, healer, counsellor, nutritionist, social worker, make-up artist, stylist, florist, party planner or hairdresser (or they may not be any of these things). If this is your life path placement, it's in your nature to create a nice, encouraging, beautiful environment in your home, family life, community and workspace for others to participate in. Without you 7s, the world would not be half as nice as it should be.

SOUL OF 8

If you have a soul placement of 8, you have access to the infinite life force of the universe. You are powerful and vigorous. You bring enthusiasm and light to any situation. When you come into the power of your 8 soul correctly and wisely, it'll fortify and charge your life, and enable you to inspire, empower and motivate others. Someone with a soul of 8 is happy when they can serve and heal. They are tapped into their prana (breath) and can create more energy through the breath. Open up to this power. Open up to fearlessness. Open up to the infinitely expansive energy of 8. You have the ability to recharge and regenerate. If you feel drained and empty, know that you can plug that battery back in. How are you directing this energy? Whatever you put your energy into can grow and flourish. It is important to do the work.

KARMA OF 8

If you have a karma placement of 8, it may be that you struggle with energy, fatigue and burnout. A deficiency of 8 can mean you become an overextended workaholic, exhausting your resources and energy. Look at what's giving your life more energy, and what is taking energy away from your life. Hold it steady. It's all about being prepared – financially, energetically and practically. Anything you put your 8 energy towards can be vital. What are you doing to make yourself vital? The number 8 has a lot of energy. It needs to take action. Through the process of applying energy, you will start to figure it out. Examine areas in your life where you overextend yourself. When we dissipate our life energy, we dissipate a lot of ourselves. You'll see how this all ties in to your general power and function in the world. When you come into the security and mastery of the number 8, you will attain a greater fearlessness.

GIFT OF 8

If you have a gift placement of 8, you're naturally energised, powerful and fearless. You have easy access to sustainability and the infinite life force of the universe. You keep going and going without necessarily burning out or getting fatigued. A gift of 8 brings a natural enthusiasm and zeal that inspires others. Your battery is charged and you're ready to motivate. Whatever you put into your projection and intention, you have the resources and life force to make it happen. This is a regenerative power: you have the energy to tap into it and apply it to any situation. Use your gifts wisely.

EXPERIENCE OF 8

If you have an experience placement of 8, you have spent many lifetimes as a healer and being of service to others. Use the powerful, fearless and positive energy of 8 in all of your experiences to continue helping the world. Allow it to be easy and natural for you.

LIFE PATH OF 8

If you have a life path placement of 8, take the road of fearlessness, power and being of service to the betterment of the planet. Use your incredible energy as a regenerative, sustainable and rebuilding force in the world. Since the energy of 8 is the healing life force, it can often manifest in many different professions, such as a doctor, producer, personal trainer, etc. Whether the number 8 manifests itself as an actual healer or not, know that it is your job to go into every situation and improve it, to make things better, bigger and infinitely inspiring.

SOUL OF 9

If you have a soul placement of 9, you are, at your truest essence, a mystic. The mystic has access to the subtle and unseen realms of all existence. Someone with a soul of 9 is incredibly graceful, intuitive, intelligent and psychic. If you have a soul of 9, it is important that you come into this refined sophistication. You have a sense of deeper hidden realms, and the ability to assess that which is not seen. People with this soul placement carry a wonderful dreaminess and passion for the inner realms, where one can gain mastery and proficiency over something that others may find mysterious. The number 9 is intricate and complex. It is a quick learner. Someone with a soul of 9 holds a very delicate yet powerful space, with the ability to figure anything out. If your soul number is 9, know that you have the ability to be a master of all systems.

KARMA OF 9

If you have a karma placement of 9, it's possible that you're way too sensitive and you really let it bog you down. You may see one little flaw in something and turn a mole hill into a mountain, create a totally distorted sense of reality, and then make neurotic decisions based on this illusion. Allow yourself to be sensitive. It's a great power, not a curse. However, just because you can read into almost any situation or get an assessment of what's happening or how people are, remember it's not all about you. When you use your 9 energy appropriately, you're elegant, intelligent and sophisticated. In other interpretations, a karma of 9 can appear as the opposite of these things. Know that you have the ability to understand and interpret any system in any situation presented before you.

GIFT OF 9

If you have a gift placement of 9, it means this number's qualities of mastery, sophistication, elegance, grace and intelligence should come easily to you. It is a very psychic number, so this is a very intuitive placement. It's your gift to be a mystic. Turn these gifts on, explore them and become a master of all systems. This could lead you to become an IT expert, a psychic, a numerologist, a writer, a race-car driver, a musician ... whatever it is, it is your gift to figure it out and make it easy. Use your gifts wisely.

EXPERIENCE OF 9

Having an experience placement of 9 basically means you're really good at being good at stuff. You've spent lifetimes figuring it out, and now you have easy access to it all. If you have an experience of 9, you can master systems very quickly, using your sensitivity and intuition to see the unseen. As you have access to these underlying patterns, you are tapped into the very intelligent, highly attuned hidden language of the universe.

LIFE PATH OF 9

If your life path placement is 9, take the road of mastery and proficiency. The Magickal teaching is to embrace and do everything with the highest degree of excellence, and by taking this approach – whether you're washing dishes or brushing your teeth – other opportunities will show up for you. You will become more limitless because nothing seems like an obstacle. As 9 is the number of mastery and systems, in a life path placement it can often manifest as many different professions, including detective, conductor, IT expert, musician, intelligence analyst, data engineer, scientist, doctor, mathematician, ghostbuster, ballerina or psychic. Stay in your grace, mystery, high intelligence and sophistication. You are a smooth operator.

SOUL OF 10

If you have a soul placement of 10, it is important that you stay in that highly-charged, energetic, radiant energy field. There's no more hiding in the shadows for you. Since 10 is your soul number, you should become comfortable with putting yourself in positions where you're seen. It is your soul's mission to bring light and greatness to the world. You have to share your talents. This is the essence of who you are. The highest essence of a 10 soul is to stand in a very strong, radiant space of spiritual nobility. Through that radiance, you have access to all prosperity.

KARMA OF 10

If you have a karma placement of 10, you could have a tendency to hide in the world. The number 10 has an 'all or nothing' energy field. Don't fall into the mindset of thinking that if you're not in first place, you're in worst place. Sometimes, people with a karma of 10 avoid putting their neck out there for fear of being ridiculed. Behaving in a way that's petty and insecure is a great dishonour to the number 10. Someone with this karma placement might feel that they should be doing something bigger and greater, and wonder why this is not happening. Remember, it takes practice to stand in that greatness. If you have a karma of 10, it's time to shine. This is one of your greatest lessons in this incarnation.

GIFT OF 10

If you have a gift placement of 10, it's generally easy for you to be in the spotlight. When you walk into a room, everybody notices you. People will be drawn to you and attracted to you. Your gift is staying in a very dignified, honourable, noble space. Show up in every situation as your biggest, most dynamic, greatest, most authentic self. When you do that, your natural alignment and leadership will come into play. Use your gifts wisely.

EXPERIENCE OF 10

If you have an experience placement of 10, you have spent many lifetimes as a person who is comfortable with being seen or holding a level of status in the spotlight, whether that's as a celebrity, politician, star waiter or team leader. It's important that someone with an experience of 10 holds a large space with dignity and humility. As you may have experience with the negative trajectory of 10, there is a chance that you have had a past life where you were ridiculed while holding a position of status and power. This is where someone with an experience of 10 might be reluctant to own their greatness, all based on a past-life trauma. Shine your light so that others may see and shine their own.

LIFE PATH OF 10

If you have a life path placement of 10, it's time to come out of hiding. Don't be afraid of your royal courage. There is a yogic teaching that says 'All prosperity comes from radiance.' Remember, the number 10 is the radiant body. If this is your life path placement, you should be able to flip the 'on' switch at any time. It's not uncommon for someone with a life path of 10 to be put in the spotlight when it comes to their job or career. This is who you are. At its core, 10 is actually a very humble number. When you shine your light on to the world, you will warm and illuminate and encourage others to come into their own greatness. This is the path you must walk.

SOUL OF 11

If your soul placement is 11, you are capable of almost anything. You are in your happy place when you act as a conduit for the infinite. You have access to so many options and possibilities. It's important to set an intention and direction, while simultaneously letting the universe take you there without getting sucked in the undertow. Your words have tremendous impact and when you have a soul of 11, it means that everything you do expands out to the world. Your vibration and frequency want to be shared. In general, the frequency of the number 11 grows and expands. When you are in flow with the infinite, you can make more things happen. It is important not to let the powerful currents of this number catch you in their undertow, leaving you feeling overwhelmed by life. Remember: the number 11 is the sound current, and sound is vibration. The number 11 is like throwing a stone into water: it ripples outward and amplifies.

KARMA OF 11

If you have a karma placement of 11, you may, at times, feel a little stagnant. Someone with a karma of 11 may be something of a spiritual vagabond, rather neglectful and lazy. It's important to know that you have a frequency that should always be expanding out and getting bigger. When you have access to all these other realms and dimensions, you may feel a sense of overwhelm and futility. There's an existential malaise that can bog down those with a karma of 11. It's important to know that you can easily tap into your flow and zone. If you have this karma placement, you need to step up and start putting things into action and motion. Get your head above water and start swimming. Start making decisions and come into your destiny. Manifest through your words.

GIFT OF 11

If you have a gift placement of 11, you have easy access to the infinite possibilities of a vibrational frequency that wants to be shared with the world. It is important to expand and grow. If you have a business, or are, for example, a writer or an investor, use your talents to make the universe work for you. That's one of the great gifts of the number 11. You have the gift of walking into the infinite opportunities and grace. A gift of 11 will naturally take on a life of its own and give back. What do you love to do? You have access to many layers of the universe. The number 11 can also be a very high teacher. Give it a little bit of time, a little bit of work, and you'll become known for your gifts. Your ideas, frequencies and energies can be seen, and can influence many.

EXPERIENCE OF 11

If you have an experience placement of 11, you have spent lifetimes accessing the vast, infinite resources of the universe. It should be easy for you to create and share your gifts and talents with the world. You have experience with expanding anything you put your energy into.

LIFE PATH OF 11

If you have a life path placement of 11, you have to get more content out into the world. You should be creating and producing and working on things to put out there. Someone with an 11 life path can have access to a very high genius in the form of divine and infinite inspiration. The universe is ready to serve you if you are able to just be you. It is your path to always have a greater experience of yourself. As you start to put this into action, you will see that the inertia of the universe will work in your favour. This is an influential life path number, where your voice can be heard by many and you have the power to amplify and expand.

GIFT OF 0

Someone with the gift placement of 0 has a natural ability to transcend any limitations. Through this shuniya state (see page 136), you have the ability to experience and understand anything. You have access to deep universal intuition. This number is very mystical because it is both a number and not a number. It exists, and it doesn't exist. It is very inter-dimensional. You have a talent with hidden mysteries. Someone with a gift of 0 transcends time and space to exist in this pure state of non-existence. There is no separation. You have access to your purest, truest, most unadulterated state. There is an innocence. It is you at your highest you. This is a gift of innovation. The number 0 is the primordial point of creation. What are you creating? What are you innovating? What would absolute stillness give you? Your consciousness has access to a realm that can transcend time and limitations, enabling you to tap into something and figure it out. You have no obstacles. You have access to the most sublime consciousness. Use your gifts wisely.

ABOUT THE AUTHOR

Remington Donovan is a master numerologist and mystic seer, trained in the spiritual wisdom of the ancients. He was quite literally born into the traditions of mysticism, spirituality and meditation, which naturally evolved into his now 30 years of experience practicing with tarot and numerology. Along with performing thousands of private readings, Remington teaches and speaks all over the world. He hosts The Mystical Artists podcast and leads The Mystical Arts Mystery School. Remington takes great joy in the gift of seeing life's highest potential through numerology and in using that gift to guide and transform others. Remington lives in Los Angeles with his wife, Jeana, and their pet crystals, where he uncharacteristically shows up on time and unironically believes in the infinite possibilities of the universe.

ACKNOWLEDGEMENTS

I would like to thank my amazing cosmic partner and wife, Jeana, whose focus, guidance, and belief in me and this work has made so much of it possible. You are a huge blessing, and without you, I would be totally screwed.

A deep humble gratitude to my teachers, seen and unseen. Your wisdom, teachings, and encouragement have made me the man I am today.

To the wonderful team the universe has conspired to put together, thank you Eve, Amelia and Bonnie for making this book so fluid and beautiful.

And for those who are still sick and suffering, know that miracles happen.

INDEX

Published in 2021 by Hardie Grant Books,
an imprint of Hardie Grant Publishing

Hardie Grant Books (London)
5th & 6th Floors
52–54 Southwark Street
London SE1 1UN

Hardie Grant Books (Melbourne)
Building 1, 658 Church Street
Richmond, Victoria 3121

hardiegrantbooks.com

British Library Cataloguing-in-Publication Data. A catalogue
record for this book is available from the British Library.

Numerology
ISBN: 978-1-78488-463-5

10 9 8 7 6 5 4 3 2 1

Publisher: Kajal Mistry
Commissioning Editor: Eve Marleau
Design and Art Direction: Amelia Leuzzi
Illustrations: Bonnie Eichelberger
Copy-editor: Tara O'Sullivan
Proofreader: Caroline West
Indexer: Vanessa Bird
Production Controller: Nikolaus Ginelli

Colour reproduction by p2d
Printed and bound in China by Leo Paper Products Ltd.